White Parents, Black Children

White Parents, Black Children

Experiencing Transracial Adoption

Darron T. Smith,
Cardell K. Jacobson, and
Brenda G. Juárez

ROWMAN & LITTLEFIELD
Lanham • Boulder • New York • London

Published by Rowman & Littlefield
A wholly owned subsidiary of The Rowman & Littlefield Publishing Group, Inc.
4501 Forbes Boulevard, Suite 200, Lanham, Maryland 20706
www.rowman.com

Unit A, Whitacre Mews, 26-34 Stannary Street, London SE11 4AB

First paperback edition published 2017

British Library Cataloguing in Publication Information Available

Library of Congress Cataloging-in-Publication Data

The hardback edition of this book was previously cataloged by the Library of Congress as follows:

Smith, Darron T., 1965–
White parents, black children : experiencing transracial adoption / Darron T. Smith, Cardell K. Jacobson, and Brenda G. Juárez.
p. cm.
Includes bibliographical references and index.
ISBN 978-1-4422-0762-2 (cloth : alk. paper) — ISBN 978-1-4422-0764-6 (electronic) — ISBN 978-1-4422-0763-9 (paperback)
1. Interracial adoption—United States. 2. African Americans—Race identity. 3. Racism—United States. 4. Race awareness in children—United States. 5. United States—Race relations. I. Jacobson, Cardell K., 1941– II. Juárez, Brenda G., 1967– III. Title.
HV875.64.S628 2011
362.734089'96073—dc23

2011030667

∞™ The paper used in this publication meets the minimum requirements of American National Standard for Information Sciences—Permanence of Paper for Printed Library Materials, ANSI/NISO Z39.48-1992.

Printed in the United States of America

Contents

Foreword

ONE OF the most generous things that people can do is take significant responsibility for other people's children. This generosity can be seen in many areas of society, but especially in the actions of caring parents who adopt displaced children who otherwise might not have homes with caring parents. In recent decades the United States has seen an increase in such adoptions, including adoptions across international and racial boundaries. One of the situations that has become much more common in U.S. society is that of transracial adoptions. These transracial adoptions most often involve relatively affluent white parents adopting children of color.

This book deals centrally with the contemporary societal reality of white parents adopting African American children. The authors draw on statistical data from surveys and on in-depth interviews with white adoptive parents and adopted African American children. After a useful statistical overview of adoption patterns, the authors systematically examine the experiences and perspectives of adoptive parents and adopted children in transracially adoptive families.

As we read and digest their data, we gain much insight not only into transracial adoptions but also into the ways in which racist realities are still central to U.S. society. One key set of findings here relates to how white parents teach black children about racial matters. These parents do give racial lessons to their adopted children. They often secure items like black dolls and books for their children. Yet, the parents rarely secure the kind of materials and instruction that they need for themselves to learn about their own racism and that of this highly racist society.

The white parents do generally teach their adopted children to be proud of their backgrounds and to have a positive sense of self-worth, but, as the authors underscore, the white parents also communicate, consciously and unconsciously, a quite different lesson that privileges white framing, characteristics, norms, and ways of doing and being. In effect, their black children are taught that whiteness is normal and that they should mostly conform to the contours and requirements of that whiteness.

The authors make clear that they are not primarily blaming white parents for their parenting styles. Instead, these researchers have examined what it means to adopt and love a black child within a society fundamentally grounded in white-imposed racism. One major goal of this book is to examine how this systemically racist society operates from the vantage point of these white parents and their adopted black children. White adoptive parents are seriously handicapped by operating out of the dominant white racial frame, which they did not invent but which they regularly operate out of, and typically with little critical awareness of its significance or impact on them. As a result, most white parents are not only unprepared to raise black children, but often unconsciously or half-consciously racist in their everyday operations and actions in regard to their children, because they too operate out of the dominant racial frame.

Discriminatory racial barriers remain significant for black progress in this supposedly postracial society. The effects of systemic racism and the white racial frame with its rationalizing antiblack attitudes are stubbornly resilient. This white racial frame is deeply embedded in everyday life and is still found shaping everyday discrimination in many societal settings, from widespread housing and job discrimination to the renewed segregation that is obvious in our mostly black and brown prison-industrial complex (Feagin 2010a). African American parents are quite familiar with the racial perils awaiting their children, which is why black children are often taught in black homes to be aware of the many pitfalls of continuing white discrimination in these various areas and how to "act" around white people. For many black families, teaching the children to know these counterframed strategies and to be proud of their black history and heritage has been a matter of individual, family, and group survival through fifteen generations now in North America (Feagin 2010a). Additionally, black childcare advocates have often spoken on the importance of teaching black children the necessary coping and resistance strategies to endure the continuing onslaught of everyday racism, which is necessary in a still-racist society to promote healthy self-esteem (Feagin 2010b). However, in the case of the increasing number of domestic transracial adoptions, little is known yet about whether white parents have similar concerns about the racial discrimination that their black adopted children will certainly encounter. The authors here have uncovered some of the usually unintentional negative consequences of much white parenting, especially when parents fail to broach the subject of white racism and to recognize its dramatic salience in the present and future lives of their adopted black children.

Early on, the authors discuss the commonplace idea that white people know little about issues of racism, yet their interviews reveal that whites know a great deal about U.S. racism, and indeed implement much racism themselves. The data in this book show that these parents regularly think, act, and interact out of what I have called the *white racial frame*, an old and continuing racial framing of U.S. society (Feagin 2010b). The contemporary white racial frame has many racial elements that date back centuries, including both pro-white stereotypes and imagery and antiblack stereotypes and imagery.

One element the authors underscore is the individualism that most white parents accent in regard to racial matters, for the dominant white racial framing they accept has regularly excluded a recognition of the reality of well-institutionalized and foundational racial oppression. As the white parents signal in their interviews, for them racism is only about individual prejudices and stereotypes, acts of meanness directed at people of color, and thus most believe firmly that blacks and other people of color are just as "racist" as whites. One central goal of the old white frame is to blame whatever intergroup "problems" exist on people of color—and not on whites or the white-run system of racial oppression. Most parents hold to this individualistic viewpoint, including the reactionary notion of *reverse racism*—a term and concept created in the 1970s by white intellectuals and other whites as part of the backlash against the 1960s civil-rights movement and the desegregation changes it brought. Another element of the contemporary white racial frame seen in the parental interviews asserts that blacks are now equal to whites, and that whatever societal racism there once was is now dead.

One difference between the contemporary white racial frame and the white racial frame under Jim Crow segregation or slavery is that it is more sensitive to being called out for still blatantly racist antiblack stereotypes, images, and narratives. These stereotypes, images, and narratives are today often covered by a thin veneer of color-blind deception on the part of many whites, who commonly make such assertions as "I don't see race," "I am not racist," or "whites are not racist any more." Such assertions are actually a form of colorblind lying and conscious misrepresentation because most whites who make them know at some level that they do indeed "see race" and think or act in racist terms. The data are quite substantial that indicate most whites—especially in backstage settings with white friends and relatives—participate in, support, and/or tolerate blatantly racist performances by other whites (see Picca and Feagin 2007). The color-blind-deception version of the white racial frame many white adoptive parents and many other whites utilize today mostly rejects blatantly racist commentary and actions in the more public frontstage settings, yet it still contains many of the old pro-white and antiblack stereotypes, images, and narratives that date back centuries.

The consequences of the white parents operating out of this white racial frame are quite serious for their children. Not surprisingly, given our deeply racist society, the black adopted children reported to the authors significant levels of everyday racial discrimination directed at them by whites, including subtle, covert, and blatant discrimination. Yet, sadly enough, most of the white parents tended to play down the discrimination reported by their children, thereby adding harm on top of harm. Another sad impact of this white framing in parents' heads is the direct impact it has had on their adopted children, many of whom frequently view the world from this pro-white, individualistic, meritocratic, non-institutional framing of society. The adopted children thus often prize whiteness and feel much pressure to think, talk, and act in white-normed and white-sanctioned ways.

In contrast to these adopted black children, most black children learn how to cope with the inevitable racist environments by interacting with and learning from their black parents and relatives. At the least, most get some significant black counter-framing against racism, which is necessary so black children can learn to cope with everyday racism. Research cited by the authors shows that most black parents teach their children about white racism and about their own racial identities, and about being proud of their racial identities. Over the centuries, African Americans have done, as many often say, "what they had to do just to survive." In this way, they have developed a counter-frame with a strong understanding of whites and white racism, and a strong dose of black pragmatism, a practical perspective that assists in dealing with everyday-racism situations. African Americans do not learn the antiracist counterframe from the mainstream media. The black counterframe is most centrally taught in African American families, with the support of African American churches and community organizations. Honest instruction and accurate socialization in regard to white racism is also substantially honed out of black parents' own lengthy experiences with racism, something most white parents cannot draw on. As the authors demonstrate well, African American children must learn about the harsh and persisting reality of white racism and how to effectively counter it if they are to survive and thrive, and they can best learn such from African American parents and other African Americans who have learned from long and hard experience about the complex realities of continuing white racism.

A strong finding from this book is that few white Americans, including those who adopt children of color, have the desire and ability to undertake a critical examination of the racially oppressive society they and their ancestors have created and maintained now for four centuries. Most whites, including these parents, act routinely out of a white racial framing, and thereby constantly reinforce it in their own minds and those of their adopted and birth children. Given the character of systemic racism and the unwillingness of most whites to seriously learn about and face such racism and its impact on black Americans, the authors correctly conclude that it is difficult for white parents, no matter how loving and well-intentioned they are, to raise black children to develop healthy self-identities and the necessary counter-framed strategies for coping with this still extraordinarily racist society. To do this, parents need to make a major commitment to social justice and a concerted effort to unlearn the dominant white racist frame that shapes their lives consciously and unconsciously.

Almost no white parents in this book seemed interested in learning a strong antiracist counterframing, including the powerful black counterframe. As a result, their adopted black children do not learn how to cope well with the everyday white racism they inevitably face in society. Those few white parents who did undertake this difficult task of learning an antiracist framing of society were the ones who were likely to get themselves and their children involved in black communities, to study and teach black history and culture to their children, and to honestly counter racist events in their children's experience. Their children, in turn, were more likely to have secure black identities. Yet these white parents are so few that they in fact prove the major theses of this important research book.

Given this sobering reality, one can understand why the National Association of Black Social Workers (NABSW) has regularly asserted its view that black children generally suffer greatly in out-of-home placements, including transracial adoptions. One can also understand why the NABSW website currently has this strong presentation (www.nabsw.org/mserver/PreservingFamilies.aspx) on the actions necessary to "Preserving African American Families" in this difficult society:

1. stopping unnecessary out-of-home placements;
2. reunification of children with parents;
3. placing children of African ancestry with relatives or unrelated families of the same race and culture for adoption;
4. addressing the barriers that prevent or discourage persons of African ancestry from adopting;
5. promoting culturally relevant agency practices; and,
6. emphasizing that transracial adoption of an African American child should only be considered after documented evidence of unsuccessful same race placements has been reviewed and supported by appropriate representatives of the African American community.

This very clear message from African American professionals speaking from their own experience and the experience of millions of African American parents has yet to be listened to and heard by most white Americans, including white parents and powerful policymakers.

Joe R. Feagin
Texas A & M University

Acknowledgments

BOOKS ARE seldom the result of one or even three people's work. That has been the case with this book. Thus, we thank the following individuals for their sagacious efforts and assistance in bringing this manuscript toward completion.

First, we thank the participants in the study who so freely gave their time, thus allowing us to capture the complexities of transracial adoption. This book would not have been possible without their participation.

We also thank Joe Feagin for writing the foreword to the book, for his encouragement, and for his exemplary and influential work on race and ethnic relations in the United States. His work has been an inspiration for all of us.

Sarah Stanton, as the acquisitions editor, has been an excellent, supportive, insightful, and gentle critic. Holly Belnap, McKenzie Mann, Camille Moss, and Camie Schiel helped us corral references.

A portion of chapter 1 draws from a paper by Brenda Juárez that was presented at the annual meeting of the Association of Black Sociologists in August 2010, entitled "Race in the Homeplace When Parents Are White and Children Are Black: Considering Transracial Adoption and Democratic Possibilities within the Racial Status Quo." Portions of chapters 5 and 6 draw from the paper "Collard Greens, Southern Ladies' Cookbooks, and Stuff on Martin: Exploring Citizenship and Minority Rights through Transracial Adoption," presented by Brenda Juárez in February 2010 at the annual meeting of the National Association of African American Studies (NAAAS); and the paper "Race Lessons Out of Context: When Whites Teach Blacks about

Racism," presented by Darron Smith and Brenda Juárez in February 2009 at the NAAAS annual meeting.

Andrea Hardeman and Leila Nielson helped with the analysis of the census and National Survey of Adoptive Parents data presented in chapter 2. We thank them.

Tasha and Marjorie Sabino read many drafts of the manuscript and offered editorial support. We thank them.

Darron Smith thanks his daughters (Keisa and Eagan Smith) for their unconditional love and inspiring strength in the face of the challenges they face daily; I love you girls and want you to have and demonstrate a healthy identity. Cardell Jacobson thanks his wife for her constant support and their ongoing life together. Brenda Juárez thanks her six children and one new daughter-in-law for their continued willingness to be patient while "Mommy's typing" and their unflagging enthusiasm for each new research project she takes on.

And may the world be a better, less racist place for all of our children and grandchildren.

CHAPTER ONE

Transracial Adoption

Considering Family, Home, and Love and the Paradoxes of Race Matters

I always felt like I had this "A" on my forehead, this adoptee, that people could see from a far distance that I was different.

—Black male transracial adoptee (Clemetson and Nixon 2006)

If we lived in a different neighborhood, I'd feel more comfortable. People wouldn't ask so many questions or call me names. I feel a little more comfortable around people who are my same color because I know they won't call me names.

—Black male transracial adoptee (De Haymes and Simon 2003, 261)

It was painful because while I perceived racism all around me, I didn't have people around me to talk to who had experienced what I was experiencing, and who could therefore validate and share my perceptions. . . . I sensed it at school, in the Eurocentric curriculum that excluded a multicultural perspective. I sensed it among my peers. I felt it from the fathers of the white girls I was interested in. I sensed it from prospective employers when I was job hunting, and from security guards in shopping mall stores, and from police who watched me and sometimes stopped me on the streets. I detected it in the comments and jokes that went unchallenged among friends, and even among members of my family.

—Black male transracial adoptee (Raible 1990, 16)

THESE THREE quotes are typical of comments regularly made by transracial adoptees, African Americans[1] who were adopted during childhood and raised by White parents, often in predominantly White communities. Although a rare occurrence throughout most of U.S. history and into the 1960s (Freundlich 2000), the numbers of transracial adoptions have been increasing at a rapidly accelerating pace since then (Smith et al. 2008; Lee 2003). In this book, we explore in detail some of the contributing factors and important consequences surrounding the growing popularity of transracial adoption.

Transracial adoption refers to a family-formation practice of joining together racially different adoptive parents and children (Silverman 1993). In the United States, most domestic transracial adoptions involve White adoptive parents and either a monoracial Black child, or a biracial child of Black heritage in combination with another ethnic, usually White, heritage. *Domestic adoptions* are those that entail the adoption of a child born in the United States.

The adoption of Black children by White parents tends to be the most controversial form of adoption, usually generating highly charged polemics and strong resistance from within the Black community. Reflected by popular movies such as *Losing Isaiah* (1995), *Antwone Fisher* (2002), and, more recently, *The Blind Side* (2009) and in talk shows and special feature articles (Samuels 2009), powerful emotions are often evoked even at the mere mention of transracial adoption. There is an adoption dilemma in these films—does race matter? As Gina Samuels (2009, 80) explains, "The most publicly debated and emotionally contentious issues in adoption policy and practice are those related to race." Why does transracial adoption incite this high degree of heated controversy in our society?

In a nation where there were once miscegenation laws strictly and often violently enforced, especially in cases of unions between Blacks and Whites, what does transracial adoption say about us as a society? Is the fact that White parents are now adopting Black children in growing numbers proof that, indeed, we have arrived at this experiment called a democracy based on equality and that racism is finally a vestige of our ugly but distant past?

We introduce the topic of transracial adoption by using broad strokes to paint a word picture that outlines the important contours, components, and controversies that have surrounded and helped to make up this particular family type. We try to share with the reader a taste of the rich and multiple dimensions of transracial adoption as these dynamics have played out on the ground in the very real lives of actual individuals and families, rather than in the often abstract theory and philosophy of textbooks and debates. The families and individuals whose stories are mentioned in this chapter are discussed in detail in upcoming chapters.

Transracial Adoption and the Competing Meanings of Race in the United States

What does transracial adoption mean for and in our society today? According to surveys on White racial attitudes, in the past three decades there has been an overall decrease in the number of Whites who subscribe to the explicitly racial views associated with old-fashioned racism (Jim Crow)—that housing and jobs, for example, should (remain and) be separate. However, the number endorsing such items still remains high, ranging from 20 to 50 percent depending on the stereotype, as evidenced by Whites' responses to survey questions saying that Blacks tend to be lazy and unmotivated and complain about racism too much (Bonilla-Silva 2003). At the same time, there has been a significant increase in Whites' acceptance of democratic ideals and equal rights for Blacks and other people of color.

Does transracial adoption thus serve as the evidence that as a nation we have finally become truly blind to color and, therefore, equal? Is race finally irrelevant? Many people in the United States want to believe so, and even more hope so.

We Are All Getting Along Now

The recent spate of high-profile Black-White transracial adoptions by Hollywood celebrities does seem to suggest that, yes indeed, the United States has finally moved into a postracial society and thus realized its democratic promise and potential by having eliminated race as a primary factor in determining an individual's life chances. In the May 10, 2010, edition of *People*, for example, reflecting the transracial-adoption trend in Hollywood, movie star Sandra Bullock was featured in the cover-story spread inviting the world to "Meet my baby!" The new adoptive mom, of course, is White, and her newly adopted son is African American.

In the paragraphs of the magazine's feature story, Bullock is quoted as saying, "We began the process . . . about four years ago, never thinking about what [the child] would look like . . . we somehow knew the right person would come" (Heyman and Chiu 2010, 172). She does not mention race or racism in this statement, or anywhere throughout the featured story, except to say that race was not considered an important factor in the adoption process. In fact, race was so unimportant that Bullock and her family seemingly never thought about it. Ironically, though, the statement—as if in response to an unspoken question—that race was "not thought about" in the adoption process seems to point to, and even underscore, the conclusion that race was contemplated, albeit unconsciously, in the thought process about adoption, and that race did, in fact, matter. Why else point out that race wasn't considered, unless it was considered?

From the excerpts included in the story, however, it also appears that during the interview Bullock was not asked any questions about race by the interviewers who wrote up her story. Questions about how the popular actress will raise her son to be a Black man in America or why there was yet another Black child in need of adoption do not appear to have emerged during the interview. Nor, apparently, were they considered important enough to be noted for future consideration and included in the published version. Apart from the hint about what the child looks like in Bullock's quoted statement and the photographs included in the article, the historically significant matter of race is strikingly absent from the story on Bullock and her newly adopted Black son.

Yet the absence of any direct or substantive mention of the matters of race and racism in the story about Sandra Bullock and her transracially adopted Black son may not be very surprising. Research on racial attitudes and perspectives has shown that White people usually don't consider matters of race and racism in their talk, interactions, and activities. Since the events of the civil-rights era during the 1960s, Whites have tended to view and make sense of the world around them through a colorblind, race-neutral perspective. Whites are typically taught from a very young age to ignore matters of race. Colorblindness is a learned behavior of willfully not seeing race when, in actuality, skin color is one of the first characteristics that individuals see about each other, along with other factors such as body size, gender, and able-bodiedness.

White people tend to understand the world in a way that filters out the realities of race and racism. They also tend to be less likely to have conscious and explicit knowledge about and experience with matters of race and racism. Moreover, because of the historical patterns of race relations in the United States, Whites are members of society's dominant group and, thus, typically have very little direct or explicit experience with or knowledge of what it's like to be a target of race-based discrimination and prejudices.

White people typically learn to think about race and racism, and they learn to come to terms with racial inequality as isolated acts of meanness while adhering to democratic ideals in their belief that American society has moved beyond color as a basis for opportunity and societal advancement. In other words, many White people are of the opinion that racism is a thing of the past, and that democratic ways of justice and equality have trumped old-fashioned racism, where color was a sheer indicator of irreducible differences. The ways White people make sense of race and racial matters are significant because they centrally influence the ways they act and interact with others. In this book, we consider how such ideas on racial understandings influenced the ways in which the White adoptive parents in our study went about the task of raising a Black child.

So We Are Not All Getting Along Then?

Unfortunately, as the epigraphs at the beginning of this chapter illustrate, while matters of race and racism may be nonissues for Bullock and most other White people in the United States, they remain a central factor that permeates the lives of most African Americans and other people marked as racial minorities. As a great deal of research has documented, Black children adopted into White families are not exempt from experiencing racial mistreatment and microaggressions. Of transracial adoptees, moreover, Black male children and Black youth in particular tend to experience the highest levels of race-based discrimination, hostility, exclusion, and other forms of microaggressions and mistreatment (Brooks and Barth 1999; Feigelman 2000). That matters of race and racism will be nonissues in the life of Bullock's young Black son, as they are in the life of his White adoptive mother, is, therefore, highly unlikely.

The centrality and significance of race and racism in the lives of racial minorities in the United States are readily visible across society. Black children are much more likely than their peers from any other social group in the United States to be removed from their families and placed in foster care. Black children, likewise, have lower adoption rates and take longer than children from any other racial group to achieve permanent family placements. Black male children, specifically, are likely to spend at least some portion of their lives in prison, given the current rates of incarcerating African Americans. As Peniel Joseph (2001, 54) argues, "To be born Black within the U.S. means to be disproportionately represented among the poor, the incarcerated, the unemployed, the sick, the under-educated and under-nourished; and, amongst those awaiting state-sanctioned execution on death row."

It is hardly surprising, then, that most African Americans and other people of color report issues of race and racism as highly relevant in today's world, despite the election of Barack Obama, the first African American, to the highest office in the land. As a group, Blacks tend to be cognizant of the fact that they are about three times more likely than Whites to be poor, earn about half as much money as Whites, and have a tenth of the total wealth that Whites have (Bonilla-Silva 2003). Similarly, Blacks are not unaware that they tend to receive lower-quality education and educational opportunities than Whites—even when they attend predominantly White institutions. Most Blacks are likewise not usually surprised to hear that they tend to live shorter lives and receive less access to quality health care than Whites. Overall, then, race remains a fact of daily life for Blacks, and this is no news flash to Blacks or other people of color in the United States (Munford 1996). However, for the many Whites who believe we are in a postracial society, this is indeed news.

The Racial Paradox: Race Does Not Matter, Except That It Really Does Matter

How is it possible for race and racism to be so unimportant for most White Americans and simultaneously so important in the lives of nearly all Black Americans and other racial minorities in the United States? The paradox of race in the United States, then, is this: simultaneously, race doesn't matter and yet race matters, depending on who you are. "Studies of transracially adopted adolescents and young adults have found that perceived discrimination is significantly associated with behavior problems and psychological distress" (Smith et al. 2008, 7). While race and racism may not be significant to White adoptive parents, the negative consequences of race are likely to remain relevant for Black and other children of color in transracially adoptive families.

The epigraphs at the beginning of this chapter are representative of how race matters for African American young people. The racial experiences reported by those adoptees are similar to and resonate strongly with those recounted to us by many of the African-descent young adults and their White adoptive parents whose stories are shared in this book.

Put bluntly, racial discrimination and mistreatment are very real, even today. Racial microaggressions are common occurrences that happen so regularly that they become mundane in the lives of Black adoptees, as well as for their counterparts who grow up in Black families and communities. As Paula,[2] a twenty-three-year-old African American woman who participated in this book's study, recalled, "It was just that you were fingered all the time. It was really weird. If you got into trouble, it's the Black person that did it."

Explaining further, Paula stated, "There were names called—the 'N word,' thing in the toilet, burnt chicken, and stuff like that."

The patterns of racial microaggressions most commonly recounted by the Black adoptees in this study, as reflected and represented by Paula's remarks, were race-based name-calling and jokes from White children and youth. Others included low expectations for academic success and high expectations for negative, socially unacceptable, or bad behavior from White adults. Describing a traumatic incident during their respective interviews, two of the young Black men from this study recalled being together on the courts as basketball players on the same team in high school and hearing racial epithets, including the "N word," yelled out at them from members of a largely White audience in the stands. Other instances of racial discrimination recounted by the transracial adoptees were much less dramatic, although no less harmful, given that our interview questions incited these memories sometimes many years later. Nykia, for instance, remembered, "Sometimes they would call me a 'mulatto' or say words like 'Negro' in my presence, things like that."

Pointedly, and very significantly, not all name-calling came from individuals intending to be negative or inflict hurt. Many of the racial incidents described by the Black adoptees in this study involved their friends, and oftentimes it was their close friends. Like many of the Black adoptees from this study, Tyric noted how his "buddies" would regularly invoke his racial background as a negative to tease him when he did something that was either thoughtless, not very smart, or not "cool" socially among their peer group. "I'll do something or say something and they'll be like, just jokingly, 'That must be your Black side,'" Tyric explained. It was also not uncommon for the friends of these adoptees to use the "N word" with them in a friendly and joking manner, in an expression of solidarity as frequently portrayed in popular culture as being enacted among African Americans.

Other adoptees felt they were targets of higher levels of discipline than other children. Still other adoptees spoke of being pushed toward sports and entertainment activities in high school, including football, basketball, and singing in the choir. Often rejected and exoticized[3] over hair and physical stature, many of the adoptees in our study spoke of difficulties in finding a dating partner. "I feel like a skin tone, not a person, sometimes," quipped Marcus, a Black adoptee we interviewed. Was it a coincidence that almost all of the Black male adoptees we interviewed had participated in sports at some point in their high-school careers, while the Black female adoptees tended to be part of musical groups such as choir?

There was a cost exacted from many of the adoptees for being the lone, token representative of the African American community in a largely White environment. Adoptees were frequently asked to take on the responsibility of representing the Black community. Susan explained, "I remember being in elementary school, Martin Luther King Day. 'We have an African American in our class today,' the teacher said. 'Can you please tell us how you feel about that?' I'd be sitting there going, 'I don't know. It's great. It's good. Ask me something else.'"

Ms. Brown, a White adoptive mother of an elementary-school-aged Black male child, told us one story about the challenges of being the representative of Black America that was deeply moving:

> My little boy, he's not one to have an identity crisis, but I remember one time when he stopped at the doorway. I was sitting in a chair and he was about eleven. He stopped into the doorway and then he looked back. I said, "You okay?" He said, "Yeah." And I said, "Is there anything wrong?" He said, "Ahhhhhh . . ." And he just burst into tears and he said, "I hate being Black." I pulled him over to sit on my lap and rocked him for a little while. He said, "I'm embarrassed to raise my hand because when I put it up everyone can see the color."

Being the only African American student in the classroom, this child took on the burden of representing his race whether or not he wanted to.

Ms. Brown told us about many incidents in which the challenge of being Black in a predominantly White setting involved more than the child raising a hand in class, as did the majority of White adoptive parents we talked with. On many occasions Ms. Brown had to go into the school to talk to the teacher and administrators about the level of discipline she felt was being unduly directed toward her son. The degree to which parents interpreted incidents as racist and harmful to their children determined how involved they became in intervening on their children's behalf.

Ms. Brown gave us an example of a time when she felt that simply comforting her young son at home was not sufficient.

> We had a really racist teacher who really picked on him. So when the boys were doing boy things, blowing their noses and, you know, things boys do, he was really picked out. I talked to the principal. I tried to work it through, and whatever. But I couldn't get any response. Finally, we moved him to a different school.

Ms. Brown's husband elaborated. "The first big problem was that if he said 'good morning,' they thought that was high achievement. So they didn't push him or expect anything out of him. That drove me crazy. That's the kind of racism that will kill him." We revisit different vignettes in which parents described racist encounters with other Whites, especially at school, in our discussion on race lessons (chapter 6).

Race Socialization: A Historical and Contemporary Necessity

The pervasiveness with which the Black adoptees reported being subjected to various forms of racial microaggressions is both significant and noteworthy. In the United States, many Black children are lacking the loving homes they need and want. White parents, in turn, often can and want to provide these loving homes. In the United States historically, "[s]ocial justice includes a vision of a society in which the distribution of resources is equitable and all members are physically and psychologically safe and secure" (Bell 1997, 1). Because it provides Black children with homes and access to other resources and opportunities otherwise less readily available to them, transracial adoption is increasingly popular and often seen as an immensely workable strategy for addressing race-based inequalities, helping society to realize a more democratic way for all. Love, after all, is purported to have no color.

As illustrated by the epigraphs at the beginning of the chapter and in the earlier text, however, knowing how to cope with racial discrimination and other forms of race-based microaggressions and hostilities remains a profoundly necessary life skill for Black children and youth, including those adopted into White families (Brown and Lesane-Brown 2006; Peters 1985; Stevenson 1993; Thompson et al. 2000). Moreover, Black adoptees frequently grow up in surroundings that are heavily saturated with White notions of beauty and privilege. Black adoptees therefore are enveloped in the knowledge, beliefs, experiences, interests, and histories associated with White people in the United States (Asante 2003; Scott 1992; West 2002). Consequently, Black adoptees regularly report having had to struggle to develop a strong sense of Black self-actualization, community, and belonging.

The challenges of Black transracial adoptees struggling with issues of race reveal a sobering truth about growing up in America—that class privilege and familial status do not always provide adequate protection from encounters with race and racism. The "one drop" rule still holds sway in a racialized society like the United States, maintaining that a person with "one drop" of Black blood is Black. Most African American children first become aware of and begin to learn about what it means to be Black within the home and with the family (Greene 1990). It is likewise usually under the constant tutelage of parents and others from within the Black community that Black children begin learning to grapple with the significance of White racism (Thomas and Speight 1999; Thornton 1997).

The process of teaching children to fend off the negative consequences of race while simultaneously developing a positive sense of self and history is identified in the scholarly literature on Black families and transracial adoption as race socialization (Lee 2003). *Race-socialization processes* are parenting practices distinctly identified with the Black community that were developed in response to the historical circumstances of White racism in the United States. Through race-socialization processes, many Black parents over generations have taught their children how to deal with issues of race and racism by implicitly and explicitly communicating with their children about "what it means to be a black American, what they may expect from black and white persons, how to cope with it, and whether or not the disparaging messages of the broader culture are true" (Greene 1990, 209). Unlike their counterparts raised in Black homes and communities, however, African-descent children adopted across racial lines are raised by White parents who usually do not share a sense of community with other African Americans.

Race Lessons: Teaching Children about Race and Racism

All of the adoptive parents who participated in this study, with the exception of one family, maintained that they were well aware of the range and types of race-based mistreatment experienced by their Black children, and they provided us with many descriptive examples. Importantly, it was the mundane, ordinary racial mistreatment experienced by the adoptees that the White adoptive parents were responding to when lessons about race tended to surface and be conveyed within each of the transracially adoptive families. These *race lessons*, as we call them, were taught by the adoptive parents and communicated to the adoptees: race-based messages about, and beliefs about, Whiteness and Blackness, and about how to successfully cope with the negative consequences of racism.

In doing the interviews, we uncovered a wide assortment of practices, strategies, and techniques used by the White parents to convey these understandings and directives regarding race and racism. Though more follows in subsequent chapters, Ms. Hansen, a White adoptive mother of three transracially adopted Black children, gives us a taste of the kinds of practices the families in this study typically shared with us. She explained,

> So I know you've got to learn. If you're going to do this [raise a Black child], you better learn. You better have read some books. You better have dolls of all ethnicities in your house. You better have read some books on this yourself, as well as having textbooks in the home on these sorts of things, so that they can make up their history and they can see other kids [who] are transracially adopted—books that have faces on them the same as yours and theirs.

Ms. Hansen, like many of the adoptive parents in this study, emphasized having toys, books, and other materials in her home to help her children learn about race, making it possible for them to see representations of their own faces reflected back to them in the things they played with and read about in their everyday surroundings. By playing with dolls whose faces looked like theirs, and by reading books that included people whose faces likewise looked like theirs and that told stories about their social group's history, Ms. Hansen's children learned that their racial background was something worthy of being included—included in social spaces that were otherwise all or mostly White. Ms. Hansen's emphasis on the importance of including toys and books that reflected her Black children's appearance is thus significant not only because it illustrates the practices she uses to teach her children about race but also because it highlights how the context the adoptees are daily immersed and live in tends to be permeated with the systemic privileging of images, beliefs, values, interests, experiences, and histories associated with White people.

Notice that Ms. Hansen is saying something else just as important about transracial adoption. She pointed out that not only was it necessary to have dolls and books to teach adoptees about race, but that "you better have read some books on this yourself." Referring to what other White adoptive parents should do in getting books for themselves, Ms. Hansen implies what she herself has had to do, and has done—teach herself about race. She posits that it is important not only for White adoptive parents to teach their Black children about race, but also for them to simultaneously teach themselves about race.

White adoptive parents, according to Ms. Hansen, must learn about race themselves to be able to teach their Black children about race. How do, and how should, they go about teaching themselves about matters of race and racism?

In this book, we draw on the experiences and wisdom expressed in the narratives of the now-adult Black adoptees and the White adoptive parents, like Paula and Ms. Hansen respectively, who participated in this study exploring the matter of transracial adoption in the United States and the challenges and opportunities associated with adopting across historical racial boundaries. Looking closely at the practices and approaches the White adoptive parents used to convey their race lessons, we examine the ways transracially adoptive families address issues of race and racism. Although we live in the historic era of President Obama as the first African American in our nation's White House, preparing the upcoming generation for the realities of race and racism nevertheless continues to be an important part of raising a Black child. Hence, for our study, we wanted to know what White adoptive parents do to help prepare their Black children to cope with the hurt of racism and grow up into happy, healthy, well-adjusted adults. We also wanted to know how the adoptees themselves responded to and applied what they had learned from their White parents' lessons about race. Put simply, what does race mean, and does that meaning change when parents are White and children are Black?

Race in the Home and Homeplace

It is well understood in the social sciences that the way societies classify race or ethnicity is not primarily on the basis of biological or genetic factors. Rather, race is a social construction, a social force that is "dynamic and constantly being renegotiated along boundaries of color" (Marable 1995, xiii). Historically, the concept of race emerges when social space is shared or threatens to become shared as individuals and groups (begin to) mark the boundaries for separating "us" and "them." How, then, is race created, refreshed, and enacted, and what are the consequences within the contemporary context of transracial adoption?

Race is continuously being (re)created within our society through various socialization processes. Some learn to be White. Others learn to be Black. Still others learn to identify themselves as Hispanic or Asian, or, more specifically, as Korean, Mexican, Chilean, Polynesian Islander, and so on. "Children are born neither with a concept of race nor their identity within a racial matrix. Rather, these are learned and constantly manipulated throughout one's life" (Coates 2007, 210).

At the same time, the home is one of society's most significant sites for the cultural production of race, with the family serving as a chief architect in the socialization processes of teaching children to identify and take their places within the existing racial hierarchy (Van Ausdale and Feagin 2001). Race is learned at home, and later in association with others. Parents serve as mediators of society's racial knowledge and other forms of knowledge and become primary interpreters of the existing social structure for their children.

Home is therefore more than just a physical location or structure. Moreover, as bell hooks (1990) explains, *the homeplace* in the Black community has historically also been a social space of caring, a site of resistance and liberation struggle "where Black people could affirm one another and by doing so heal many of the wounds inflicted by racist domination" (42). Black children adopted by White parents, however, learn about race in White homes, usually in predominantly White areas of society.

Reflecting the racial complexities and contradictions of contemporary society, then, transracial adoption may serve as a proxy for exploring larger issues of race and race relations in the United States. Meanings of race connect systemic patterns of inequality in U.S. society to individuals' daily lives as people enact practices and interact in ways that either build up or challenge the existing racial social order. Racial meanings, in turn, are carried within practices. We want to know not only what the White adoptive parents' race lessons are but also how those racial meanings that are conveyed within these race lessons teach adoptees to think about and act on race and the existing racial hierarchy.

Racial Equality and the Potential of Transracially Adoptive Families

In sum, the phenomenon of domestic adoptions across racial lines in U.S. society, the subject of this book, has immense potential both for fostering and for limiting the realization of racial equality. Transracial adoption is both deeply perplexing and highly interesting because race simultaneously does and does not matter. White parents who adopt transracially love their children; like most parents they want what's best for these young people, and they do the best job they can rearing them. This book is not about blaming White parents, or even suggesting their parenting is inadequate. Instead, we explore what it means to love and raise a child within the context of the American racial paradox. We look at some of the ways parental understandings about race, regardless of intentions, may serve to either challenge or build up the existing racial divide in U.S. society.

As Sharon Rush (2000), a White adoptive mother of a Black child herself, has noted, "White parents of children of color are uniquely situated to contribute to the study of the relationship between White people of goodwill and racism" (7). The bond between a parent and a child is one of the most powerful and deeply felt connections between human beings. Whereas White people in general may not feel inclined to learn about racial issues and their usually negative consequences and do something about them, White adoptive parents, through their Black children, tend to have strong vested interests in doing so.

Raising a Black child oftentimes provides the encouragement and motivation for White adoptive parents to learn at least something about issues of race and racism—sometimes the hard way, as we shall see in later pages—because they love and want the best for their children. At the same time, as we have already begun to see from the excerpted interviews in this chapter, transracially adopted Black children frequently struggle against the challenges of race and racism. The experiences of transracially adoptive White parents and Black children thus provide a fundamentally rich venue for all of us to learn more about how to effectively work against the historical boundaries of race toward true racial equality (to the extent it is possible).

Looking Forward to the Chapters Ahead

The experiences of transracially adoptive families are reflected by and carried within the stories told to us by adoptive parents and adoptees during our interviews. In the upcoming chapters, we draw on these narratives to paint a richly detailed picture of the many dimensions, dynamics, and controversies that make up and surround the matter of transracial adoption.

In the next chapter we set the stage for our exploration of transracial adoption with a statistically based overview. We use the demographic data from the 2000 U.S. Census and the National Survey of Adoptive Parents to consider how trends at the macro level continue to change family formation in our society. We investigate, for example, who adopts and why they adopt. We also look at who is being adopted and where they are being adopted from.

There are important distinctions between domestic and intercountry adoptions. As conditions abroad change, adoptive parents sometimes decide to adopt within the United States. What, we want to know, are the conditions and interests, political, economic, and otherwise, that have influenced and made possible the rapidly growing trend of transracial adoption in the United States?

Finally, in chapter 2, we introduce our interviewees—the families and individuals whose stories are included in this book. Those who are interested in an elaboration of our methods and the methodological issues associated with qualitative issues should refer to appendix A.

Next, in chapter 3, we identify and explore topics that strongly influence transracial adoption and are therefore important within this context. For example, what, if anything, do Whites know about race? If Whites know something about race, how do they learn it? It is important to know what Whites know about race and how they learn it because, after all, there would be no adoption that is transracial without the concept of race.

We then situate our examination of White racial knowledge within a brief review of the complex history of race relations in the United States. An examination of the history of race relations between Blacks and Whites is a useful endeavor because it was within this struggle that transracial adoption emerged, and it is within this struggle that it is firmly located today. We cannot understand transracial adoption at present without understanding the historical conditions that have given rise to it.

In chapter 4 we explore the three main bodies of research on transracial adoptions that currently drive the field: outcomes, racial-identity development, and race-socialization practices. Each specific body of literature has a significant piece to contribute to the overall workings of adoption studies and to this book. Our aim is to provide some background regarding the important segments that created our study.

Chapter 5 provides more detailed portraits of the adoptive parents and their particular experiences and backgrounds learning about race and racial differences. We introduce the parents' background experiences as a way to better understand how and why they taught their children about race in the ways they did. Chapter 5 sets the stage for the race lessons presented in chapter 6.

Chapter 6 is about the adoptive parents' actual race lessons. Our goal in this study was to learn how White adoptive parents went about the task of teaching their Black children about race and racism. Accordingly, in this chapter we detail some of the representative racial incidents that occurred in the lives of the adoptees and their family members and how the adoptive parents responded with lessons on dealing with race and racism.

Our final chapter, chapter 7, is a reflection of and response to our work on transracial adoption from the vantage point of a Black parent of daughters who, while not adopted, are of Black-White heritage, and who are being raised by a White mother and, in many ways, apart from their Black family members. Chapter 7 also addresses pitfalls and suggests strategies that can assist White adoptive parents in raising their children to be positive and healthy in spite of their circumstances of living in a White world.

CHAPTER TWO

Contextualizing Transracial Adoption

Demographic Trends, Introducing the Families

> They said because we already had [biological] children, chances of getting another Caucasian child were minimal, which—to us, we didn't care. We said, "You know what? We don't want a Caucasian baby. Give us any other baby." It didn't matter to us. So then we started that process and adopted our son.
>
> —Ms. Ross, White adoptive mother of three Black children

> We were thinking about an African American child, but they [the adoption agency] were slow getting back to us. . . . Did a private adoption through Colombia. China had opened up . . . we didn't qualify for China, so I came back here [to adopt in the United States]. We were looking for a girl, but we brought another boy home.
>
> —Ms. March, mother of eight adoptees, three Hispanic and five Black

MOST ADOPTIONS are not transracial adoptions. But transracial adoption has increased dramatically in recent decades. We've chosen to focus on African American children who have been adopted by White parents because these adoptions present the most salient and poignant issues, and they elicit the deepest reactions from others. In this chapter we present a brief, general history of transracial adoption. Then we introduce the families we interviewed, who are typical of others in the United States who have adopted transracially.

The increase in transracial adoptions is the result of several demographic trends in the United States, as well as some abroad. We rehearse a few here. First, approximately one in five American women now either chooses not to have children or is incapable of having her own child (Lunneborg 1999; Pertman 2000). The inability of potential parents to produce their own birth children is a major factor in adoption (Hajal and Rosenberg 1991). Other parents adopt for altruistic reasons (Berry et al. 1996). The epigraphs at the beginning of this chapter reflect these patterns and the reasons why families and individuals choose to adopt. And the number of women and men choosing to adopt remains high.

A second factor associated with increased adoption is that most families are smaller than in the past. In addition, Heather Jacobson (2008) notes that women have increasingly engaged in careers, postponed having babies, and experienced fertility problems that occur more often among couples trying to have babies at a later age. The ideal family size (expressed by prospective parents) and the actual average family size have also declined. All of these trends together have reduced the number of White babies given up for adoption. Most adopting parents are White, and they want a healthy, newborn baby that looks like them—a same-race baby. As the demographic trends have changed, however, the number of such babies has declined. So families adopt internationally or from other racial or ethnic communities within the United States, creating transracial families.

In the discussion that follows, we present data from the National Survey of Adoptive Parents (NSAP) and from the 5 percent Public Use Micro-data Samples (PUMS) of the 2000 census that examine the social and demographic characteristics of those families that have adopted transracially. Readers interested in more detailed descriptions of these data can refer to appendix B.

Here, we first describe some general trends in adoption. We then describe the demographics of those who adopt.

A Very Brief History of Adoption

Though informal adoption has occurred since ancient times, the concept of formal adoption became embedded in U.S. society only in the late nineteenth century (Zamostny et al. 2003). Historically, "baby farms" took in unwanted and illegitimate children to use as laborers, but the increasing trend of "sentimental adoption"—adopting based on the emotional value of the child—caused a decline in the social acceptance of baby farms (Zelizer

1985, 189). This change also affected the rights of adoptees, since adoption grants adoptees inheritance rights that are typically obtainable only through birth relationships (Zamostny et al. 2003).

After the mid-twentieth century, the number of transracial adoptions in the United States increased dramatically through the end of the century before declining at the end of the first decade of the twenty-first century.

The long-term trends of adoption over the past half century or more began after World War II and the Korean War. American families adopted German, Japanese, and Korean children, and the adoption of African American children into White families was in practice by the 1960s (Lovelock 2000; Lee 2003). Adoptions from Vietnam also increased after the war in Vietnam (Lovelock 2000).

These trends suggest that the stigma historically attached to adoption is increasingly less of a factor informing family-formation practices, as a growing number of prospective parents look to adoption to begin and expand their own families. Thus, the United States is presently undergoing what Sandra Patton (2000) calls a process of multiracialization of its citizenry, as the rates of interracial marriage, multiracial foster-care arrangements, transracial adoption, and international adoption all increase. Kelley Kenney (1999, 51) notes that the multiracial population is "one of the fastest growing segments of the U.S. population."[1] The increasing popularity of transracial adoption in the United States reflects this society's growing multiracial population. We now turn to a closer examination of demographic factors associated with adoption and transracial adoption.

Demographic Trends in Adoption: What Do the Numbers Say?

The United States collects massive amounts of information on its population. Three important sources of information from government statistics provide background to our interviews. The first is the Public Use Micro-data Sample (PUMS) from the 2000 census. The second is the Department of Homeland Security.

The third is the NSAP, which provides information on both families that have adopted children of their own race and those who have adopted transracially. Our purpose in presenting the inclusive data on transracial adoptions is to provide a historical, contextual background for our emphasis on the adoption of African American children by White parents.

The PUMS was used by Rose Kreider (2003) to examine the social and demographic characteristics of those who have adopted transracially, and we elaborate on her findings. Kreider's analysis shows that about 17 percent of all adopted children have a parent of a different race. And 6.6 percent of the Hispanic children in the sample do not have a Hispanic parent. The more recent data from the NSAP (Vandivere et al. 2009) shows that 40 percent of all adoptees are transracial adoptions. The NSAP also shows that 54.5 percent of the transracial adoptions are intercountry adoptions, 25 percent are from the foster-care system, and 20 percent are private adoptions.

Intercountry Adoptions

Figure 2.1 presents the trends in intercountry adoption. (The graph is taken from the Homeland Security website.) While the number of intercountry adoptions increased dramatically from 1999 to 2004, they have dropped by nearly half over the past five years. The availability of international adoptions changes as exporting countries change their laws and restrictions to come into compliance with the United Nations and U.S. guidelines and laws (the Hague Convention on Protection of Children Act, the Multiethnic Placement Act of 1994, and the Child Citizenship Act of 2000). As conditions abroad change, adoptive parents sometimes turn to domestic adoptions.

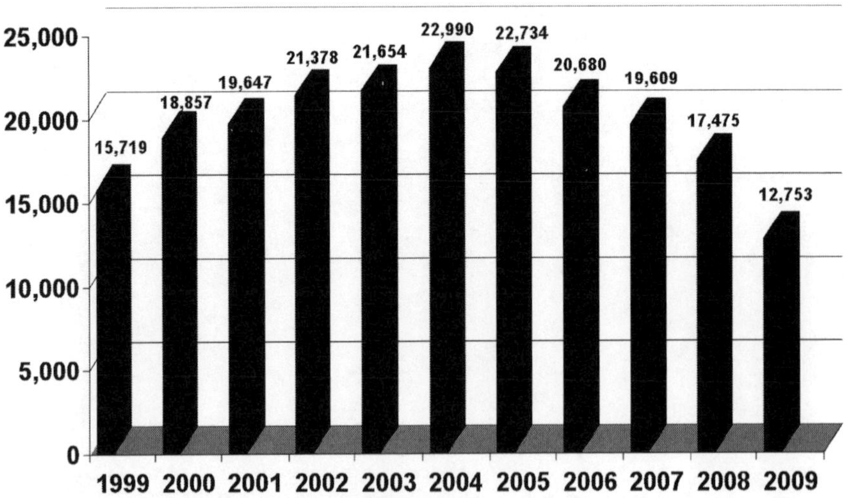

Figure 2.1. Trends in Intercountry Adoption

A large proportion of both the intercountry adoptions and those adopted within the United States are transracial adoptions.

The Department of Homeland Security tracks the number of immigrant visas issued for immigrant children (see figure 2.1). The number of foreign-born children increased dramatically from 7,093 in 1990 (including 2,620 from Korea alone) to nearly 19,000 in 2000. After 2000, the number rose to a high of nearly 23,000 in 2004 before declining to 20,680 in 2006, 19,609 in 2007, and 17,475 in 2008, and then dropping dramatically to 12,753 in 2009 and to 11,058 in 2010.

Through 2007, China was the country from which the most adoptive children came to the United States. Even so, the number of children adopted from China dropped from 7,903 in 2005 to 5,543 in 2007. By 2009, the number of adoptions from China had dropped to 3,001, but rebounded to 3,401 in 2010. Guatemala also provides a lot of children for adoption. In 2008, Guatemala provided the largest number of children for adoption, 4,122. However, the number of adoptions from Guatemala plummeted in 2009 to 756, and to 50 in 2010. The worldwide recession that began in the latter half of 2008 undoubtedly affected the number of adoptions. More importantly, however, by 2009 both China and Guatemala had imposed more stringent standards on intercountry adoptions. Beginning in May of 2007, China's official policy changed to prohibit adoption by single women, same-sex couples, heterosexual couples married less than two years, and eventually "overweight" couples. An additional factor was increased observation of the Hague Adoption Conventions. Further, some of the decline may also be due to an increasing sense of embarrassment on the part of countries such as China and Guatemala, as they are increasingly perceived as willingly relinquishing their children to other countries.

In 2008, adoptions from Guatemala and China accounted for nearly half (46 percent) of all children adopted from abroad by Americans. In 2009, the adoptions from these two countries comprised less than 30 percent. In 2010, the 3,401 children adopted from China remained the highest number of any country, followed by 2,511 from Ethiopia, 1,079 from Russia, 865 from South Korea, and 450 from Ukraine (United States Department of Homeland Security, at adoption.state.gov/about_us/statistics.php, accessed June 15, 2011). The number of adoptions from Russia also declined dramatically, from 4,631 in 2005 to 1,586 in 2009. Again, most of these intercountry adoptions, though not most of those from Russia, would be considered transracial adoptions if the children were adopted by White parents.

Data from the 2010 census are not available as we write this book, but data from the 2000 census provide additional information about transracial adoption. The census provides the largest, nationally representative sample of families that have adopted transracially. Further, the 2000 census was the first census that asked whether each child in the household was adopted or was a stepchild. Approximately 2.1 million of the total 84 million children tallied in the census were adopted (roughly 2.5 percent). The regional variations are small (2.6 percent in the Midwest, and 2.4 percent in all other regions). Whether adoptions were formal and legal or informal adoptions is not ascertained in the census data. Adoptions also include stepchildren who were adopted as a result of marriage. Nevertheless, the number of transracial adoptions in the United States is impressive.

In 2000, 13 percent of all adopted children were foreign born. Nearly half (48 percent) of the foreign-born adopted children were from Asia, a third were from Latin America, and 16 percent were from Europe. Consistent with the Department of Homeland Security data, the census data show that the percentage of adoptive children coming from Asia and Europe was increasing in 2000. (Fifty-four percent of adopted children under the age of six were from Asia, and nearly 27 percent were from Europe.) The percentage of adoptions coming from Latin America appeared to be declining in the 2000 census.

The census data also show that the percentage of adopted African American children appears to be higher than the percentage of African Americans. Approximately 16 percent of adopted children in the census are African Americans, compared to 13 percent of biological children. This corresponds with data from the foster-care system indicating that more African American children are available for adoption than are White, Asian, or Hispanic children. The same is true for American Indian and Alaskan Natives. While American Indians and Alaskan Natives together constitute 1 percent of the population, American Indian and Alaskan Native children are 1.6 percent of all adopted children (Kreider 2003).

The sex ratio of children adopted from the Asian countries is skewed. Most populations have slightly more females than males. The sex ratio for adopted Asian children in the United States is far higher: 63 percent are female. Much of this imbalance is the result of the surplus of girls from China. Ninety-three percent of the adopted babies from China in 2000 were female (Kreider 2003). Kreider argues that women, especially single women, express a preference for adopting girls. At the same time, traditional families in China have a strong preference for male children. Since China imposed its one-child-per-couple policy, female children are far more likely than male children to be given up for adoption. Asian adoptees make up 4.2 percent of all adopted children. The sex-ratio imbalance within that group is reflected in the following comparison: 54 percent are female, whereas only 46 percent are male.

Ninety percent of transracial adoptions involve White parents. Black, Asian, and Hispanic parents together account for 10 percent. Some of these may be informal adoptions by grandparents, uncles and aunts, and others. The census data do not provide that detail.

Even though regional variations in adoption are not large, the variation by states is higher. Nationally, 2.4 percent of all children in the United States under the age of eighteen are adopted. Delaware has the lowest rate (2.0 percent); then California (2.1 percent); Louisiana; New Jersey; and Texas, with 2.2 percent. Alaska is the state with the highest percentage of adoptions (4.7 percent). According to Kreider (2003), Alaska has a lot of informal adoptions. Next highest are Vermont; Oregon; and Montana, with 3.1 percent.

The percentage of Hispanic children adopted (1.8 percent) is slightly lower than the national average. All the other ethnic groups, with the exception of Whites, show higher numbers of adoptees—for example, African Americans (2.9 percent), Asians (4.2 percent), and American Indian/Alaskan Native children (4.5 percent). The percentage of Native Hawaiians/Pacific Islanders is particularly high considering the small proportion this combined group makes up of the population as a whole. Even though this group represents only four tenths of one percent of the population, almost 4 percent (3.6) of the children are adopted. This may reflect the informal adoptions present in these cultures. (See appendix B for more details on these data.) Only 11 percent of all the transracial adoptees are African American. At the same time, African American children are somewhat more likely than the national average to be adopted (2.9 percent, compared to the national average of 2.4 percent). This suggests that a lot of the adoption of Black children is by Black families, some of which is likely informal adoption.

More than one in five (23 percent) of the transracial adoptions was classified in the census as "other," "more than one race," or the Native American and Alaskan Native groups (AIAN). This percentage is more than double the size of these combined groups from the census as a whole (9 percent of the population). This higher rate of transracial adoption for these groups likely reflects several factors. First, as noted, many of the adoptions in Alaska are informal adoptions. This contributes to the high rate of adoption there.

Second, the "more than one race" category likely reflects those individuals who are biracial. Those marked as "other" may also be biracial or multiracial children. Third, many White parents express a preference for biracial children over African American children (Jacobson 2008); and finally, the small size of some groups means that many have children with spouses or partners outside their own group.

White families who adopt transracially tend to have higher income and educational levels than Whites with White children. This is true for two-parent families and for single-parent families. The educational levels are only slightly higher for those who adopt Black children (11.20 vs. 10.58 for same-race children, where 12 is completion of an associate's degree). Two-parent White families that have adopted Hispanic and Asian adoptees have substantially higher educational levels (11.64 and 12.19, respectively, compared to 10.58 for two-parent White families who have White children). The analysis yields similar, but slightly greater differences, for single-parent White families that have adopted transracially (see appendix B).

The more recent NSAP shows similar results. The NSAP uses a different measure of income than the census. It measures income in five categories, based on poverty levels. As with the census data, the NSAP data show that families that adopt transracially tend to have higher levels of income than those that adopt same-race adoptees. (See appendix B for more details.) The parents of Asian adoptees clearly have the highest income levels. Nearly two thirds (64.6 percent) of those families have incomes in the highest category of the NSAP. At the same time, those families that adopted Black children have the lowest percentage (29.7 percent) in the highest income bracket. Conversely, less than 1 percent of the families that adopted Asian children are at or below the poverty line, while 18 percent of the families that adopted Black children are in that same category.

The NSAP also shows that those who adopted transracially were slightly more likely than same-race-adopting families to have other children in the family (52 percent compared to 43 percent) and tended not to have their own biological children, compared to same-race-adopting families. These trends and data suggest that the transracial adopters waited longer to adopt.

The reasons for the economic differences in both the census data and the NSAP are not entirely clear. Two probable causes, however, are the costs of adoption and the market economy in adoption. Adopting from abroad generally is more expensive than adopting domestically. Families exercising that option probably have more disposable income, which is associated with higher educational levels. The second reason is disconcerting. As we interviewed adopting parents for background for this book, several individuals told us that African American adoptees are simply cheaper. Some agencies charge more for healthy White babies (see Jacobson 2008). As with much of American life, adoption is part of a market economy. Another possible cause for the differences, one that is connected to the relative costs of Black and White babies, is simply racism. As we noted earlier, the ideal preference for White adopting couples is a baby that looks like the adopting parents, a phenotypically White baby. As Heather Jacobson (2008) notes, a clear hierarchy exists in the adoption world. Healthy White babies are preferred. After that Asian or Hispanic children are preferred, then biracial babies, then Black babies.

Two other factors associated with adoption are prior military service and region of the country. Two-parent families where fathers have had military service are 50 percent more likely to adopt transracially than families that have not served in the military. Just over 1 percent (1.3 percent) of the parents with their own birth children have served in the military, compared to 1.7 percent of parents who have adopted either Asian or Hispanic children. Those who have adopted Black children are the most likely to have previous military service (2.1 percent). The military provides exposure to other cultures and other groups of people. It does this both within the military and in service in other countries. This exposure likely increases the willingness of military service personnel to consider transracial adoptions.

Another factor associated with transracial adoption is region of the country. While the overall rates of adoption in the census data did not vary greatly by region, the rate of transracial adoption was substantially lower in the South (22 per 10,000, compared to 37, 38, and 40 in the West, Midwest, and Northeast respectively). Some researchers (e.g., Heaton and Jacobson 2000; Johnson and Jacobson 2005) have found that the American South is significantly different from other regions of the country in levels of support for interracial marriage and actual rates of intermarriage. The social conservatism of the South and the stronger attitudes against interracial dating and marriage among southerners likely influence adoption choices for southern families as well.

Interestingly, then, most transracial adoptions are not White parents with Black children. The most common transracial adoptees are Asians (32 percent of the transracial adoptees in the NSAP), then Hispanic or Latino (27 percent), then "other" groups such as Pacific Islanders, American Indian, and Alaskan Natives (17 percent). Only 12.7 percent of all transracial adoptees are Black, and 10.6 percent are White with one or both parents from another group. Nevertheless, as we have noted, the most interesting transracial adoptions involve Black children adopted by White parents. Less racism exists with regard to Asian or Hispanic groups. And the identity issues become more prominent for African American adoptees.

Transracial Adoption Forecasted

In sum, though the number of intercountry adoptions has decreased in the last five years, the number of transracial adoptions in the United States has increased dramatically over the past several decades. Some of this increase has resulted from wars and from humanitarian efforts to attend to children that were orphaned as a result of those wars. Other reasons for the increase include the increased infertility that accompanies later-age attempts to conceive, and the decline in the availability of healthy White babies. The decline in available White babies, in turn, reflects changes in retention of babies by single parents; the increased availability of abortion; and the postponement of childbearing that has become more common as more women have had professional careers.

Increased acceptance of transracial adoption and interracial marriage and the decline of blatant prejudice are also likely factors associated with the increase in transracial adoption. Though most of the country is more accepting of interracial relationships, the South appears to be the slowest region in terms of its willingness to accept transracial adoption. The exposure of military personnel to a desegregated military and to cultures abroad is another factor associated with willingness to adopt transracially. As we shall see, however, simply having experiences with, and being in contact with, other groups of people does not mean that issues of race and racism go away.

One significant implication of the decline in the last five years in intercountry adoptions is that domestic adoptions are likely to increase. More children will likely be adopted out of the foster-care system, and more are likely to be African American adoptees. Adopting families are also likely to turn to still other countries where adoptees are available. More generally, the increases in interracial marriage and transracial adoption may lead to increased acceptance of other groups. As the family trends we have identified continue, transracial adoption will likely be an option that more families seek.

Put simply, transracial adoption is here to stay, and we can expect to see many more transracially adoptive families in our future. As the numbers of transracial adoptions continue to rise, it is imperative that we better understand the racial paradox: that "race does not matter" for many Whites, but it matters in the lives of White adoptive parents and their adopted children of color. Historically, Black-White coalitions for race-based equality consistently failed because this racial paradox was not systemically addressed or resolved (Bennett 1972). As the historical record shows (Baldwin 1985; DuBois 1940/1968), any degree of progress toward racial justice has most consistently occurred at moments in U.S. history when the collective interests of Whites converged at least momentarily with those of communities of color (Bell, 2004; Foner, 1999).

The Interviewees

We interviewed fourteen individual adoptive parents about their experiences as transracial parents. Four were couples whom we interviewed together. Three were individuals from couples no longer together, and three were individuals whose partners were not available at the time of the interview. We also interviewed thirteen adoptees who were now adults. All adoptive parents self-identified as White, and all adoptees self-identified as Black or as biracial with mixed Black-White heritage. Five of the adoptees had recently graduated from high school and were eighteen or nineteen years old. The remaining adoptees ranged from twenty-one to twenty-nine years in age. While all adoptees identified themselves as Black or biracial during interviews, three suggested that the lightness of their skin tones allowed them to be seen as nearly White or as almost "passing" for White.

With the exception of one individual who self-identified as working class, all of the adoptive parents identified themselves and their families as economically middle class. The economics and lifestyle of our sample were consistent with the results of the national studies.

Part of the explanation for the higher income and educational levels is that intercountry adoptions are expensive, requiring travel abroad. Further, the cost of adoption is itself high. However, the disparities between Asian, Hispanic, and Black children may reflect market conditions. Proportionally, more African American children are in the foster system than White children. And some agencies quite clearly have racial policies that steer some adoptive parents in particular directions.

In any case, our respondents are typically middle class, and typical of what we found in our analyses of the census and NSAP data. With the exception of one respondent, all reported having at least some college experience. Two of the adoptive parents were licensed and practicing attorneys. Two adoptive parents had acquired advanced graduate degrees, and four held bachelor degrees (see table 2.1).

In the table we present some basic information about the respondents. Note that the names, and some of the background data, have been changed

Table 2.1. Demographic and Family Profiles of Respondents

Family Name; Total Number of Children	*Race of Adoptive Parent(s)*	*Relationship Status of Adoptive Parents*	*Gender(s) of Adoptive Parent Interviewee(s)*	*Age of Adoptive Parent(s)*	*Educational Level(s) of Adoptive Parent(s)*	*SES of Adoptive Family*	*# of Adopted Children (Age Range)*	*Race(s) and Gender(s) of Adoptees*
Collins 1 child	White	No longer together	Male interviewed alone with White adopted son periodically entering and contributing	Mid- 40s	High-school graduate.	Working class	1 (high school)	Female monoracial African American
March 4 children	Both White	Together	Female interviewed alone	Both late 40s	Both hold college degrees.	Middle-class professional	4 (high school)	1 Hispanic male 2 biracial Black females 1 monoracial Black male
Brown 3 children	Both White	Together	Male and female interviewed together	Both late 40s	Both hold college degrees. Male is an attorney.	Middle-class professional	3 (1 adult, 2 middle school)	1 biracial Black female 2 monoracial Black males
White 4 children	White	No longer together	Female interviewed alone	Early 60s	Holds college degree. Former partner is an adoption attorney.	Middle-class professional	4 (all adults)	1 biracial Black female 3 monoracial Black males
Hansen 3 children	Both White	Together	Female interviewed alone	Both late 50s	Female has college experience. Male holds college degree.	Middle-class professional	3 (middle school)	1 monoracial Black female 1 monoracial Black male 1 biracial Black female

Stevens 2 children	Both White	Together	Male interviewed alone	Both early 50s	Female has college experience. Male holds college degree.	Middle-class professional	2 (1 adult, 1 middle school)	2 biracial Black males
Ross 2 children	Both White	Together	Male and female interviewed together	Both late 40s	Female has college experience. Male holds college degree.	Middle-class professional	3 (1 adult, 1 high school, 1 middle school)	1 biracial Black male 1 biracial Black female 1 monoracial Black female
West 5 children	Both White	Together	Male and female interviewed together	Both early 50s	Both have college degrees.	Middle-class professional	5 (all adults)	1 monoracial Black male 3 Korean females 1 biracial Black male
Davis 2 children	White	No longer together	Female interviewed alone	Early 60s	Holds college degree.	Middle-class professional	2 (both adults)	1 biracial Black female 1 monoracial Black female
Vest 1 child	Both White	Together	Male and female interviewed together	Both late 30s	Female has college experience. Male holds college degree.	Middle-class professional	1 (infant)	Biracial Black male

Note: Names and some descriptive information have been changed to preserve anonymity.

to preserve anonymity. Where we have changed background information, we have tried to preserve the general sense of the types of individuals who adopt transracially. Most would likely be willing to have their identities revealed, but we pledged to conceal their identities.

Note in table 2.1 that most of the adoptive parents had acquired at least some college experience and were economically stable. The ages and number of children adopted varied from family to family, as did the ages of the adoptive parents. Several of the adoptive parents adopted children of more than one racial background other than White, thus creating families that included children of Hispanic, Asian, and African descent.

The demographics of some of the Black adoptees are presented in table 2.2. Six of the adoptees were the adopted children of White parents who participated in our study. These adoptees were old enough that they could articulate their experiences. All but one had never been married. The one who had married was divorced with two children. Among the thirteen adoptees, six had been adopted as infants, and seven had been adopted as adolescents; seven of the adoptees were men, and six were women. Eleven of the adoptees had been adopted out of the foster-care system. All except one of the adoptees had been born in the United States. The other was born in Haiti.

At the time of the interviews, none of the adoptees had college experience, though all of the recent high-school graduates articulated plans to attend a university within the next two years. One adoptee had spent a year in prison, but was successfully holding down a delivery job at the time of our interview. One adoptee was a previously married mother of two children working in a governmental agency to support her family. Another adoptee was a professional basketball player on a women's team. One adoptee worked in his family's business. One was a car salesman. Most of those that had recently graduated from high school had yet to find employment (see table 2.2).

We now turn to the knowledge Whites tend to have about race. The parents we interviewed tended to have more racial knowledge than most other Whites, a knowledge gained out of their experiences as transracial adopting parents. As we shall see, however, many prospective parents believe that "love is enough."

Table 2.2. Black Adoptee Participants' Demographic Profiles

Name of Adoptee	*Race*	*Gender*	*Age at Time of the Study*	*Age at Time of Adoption*
Carl	Monoracial Black born in Haiti	M	24	14 yrs.
Damon	Monoracial African American	M	24	10 yrs.
Danielle	Biracial African American–White	F	26	7 yrs.
Darius	Monoracial African American	M	18	3 mos.
Dinesha	Biracial Hispanic–Black	F	19	9 mos.
Jamal	Monoracial African American	M	18	2 mos.
Marcus	Biracial African American–White	M	23	4 mos.
Michael	Biracial African American–White	M	29	13 yrs.
Nykia	Biracial African American–White	F	22	14 yrs.
Paula	Monoracial African American	F	23	6 yrs.
Susan	Biracial African American–White	F	26	8 mos.
Tanya	Monoracial African American	F	25	8 yrs.
Tyric	Biracial African American–White	M	18	1 mos.

CHAPTER THREE

Transracial Adoption, White Racial Knowledge, and the Trouble with "Love Is Enough"

Ms. *March* (a White adoptive mother of five Black children): I have a daughter who was raised in a very racist Black home. . . . She's very racist towards Whites. Very much; Whites were to be used. The only good thing about Whites was their money.

Darron [laughing]: I don't know if I . . . I think maybe I might agree with her. No. Just kidding. It's interesting—for her being raised in an all-White family.

Ms. *March:* Well, we're not all White, though. Whites are the minority in our family, so you can't really go there.

Ms. *White* (a White adoptive mother of four Black children): Now you talk to my son, and he'll ask you, "What's in it for me? Do I get compensated?" Because his whole thing is, "What's this world going to give me back because they've taken so much?"

Darron: Reparations?

Ms. *White:* He just has this thing. He'll say, "Mom, I love you, but I hate all other White people." Now that's very sad. I don't like that. And I tell him that is unjust.

Cardell: I think he's complimenting you.

Ms. *White:* No, because he knows too many wonderful White people. And I can [ratchet] "up" this thing. I have to say, "Well, what about that pond-scum Black guy that did this, you know?" All of us can use that.

WHAT DO White people know about race? It is often suggested, even taken for granted, that Whites do not know anything about race, or at least know very little about race, because supposedly race does not affect them. Reflecting the idea that Whites know little about race, for instance, we often hear White people in the university classes we teach make statements like, "I had never thought about myself as a White person," or "I never knew I was White before this class." Our Black students often find these kinds of expressions of White racial ignorance amusing, if very difficult for them to believe and understand.

If most Whites do not know anything or much about the racial experiences of Blacks, what about White adoptive parents? There is no adoption that is transracial without the concept of race. If White adoptive parents do know something about race, what do they know, and how did they learn it? Where does their knowledge about race come from?

As the exchange that opens this chapter illustrates, and as we will discuss further, White adoptive parents do know a great deal about race; White people do have racial knowledge, a particular kind of racial knowledge, not a lack of racial knowledge. Indeed, the interview excerpts at the start of the chapter not only showcase exactly how White people *do* have racial knowledge; the excerpts also—and this is important—showcase how they draw on and *use* that racial knowledge to make sense of the world around them. The two White adoptive mothers in the excerpted interviews use their knowledge about race to decide that the negative responses their Black children have voiced to them about White people are not appropriate.

In this chapter we examine the idea that White people do not know much about race and how White racial ignorance can influence transracially adoptive families. Whites do know a great deal about race, both in its everyday forms and in its structural sense as a system of race-based practices that privilege the interests, values, experiences, histories, and beliefs associated with White people. We use Whiteness theory and Joe R. Feagin's (2010b) notion of White racial framing to explore what White people know about race, how they learn about it, and what the consequences are. We then situate this White racial knowledge within the historical context of U.S. race relations to briefly trace its development over time. By exploring what White people know about race and how race is enacted in the everyday lives of families, it becomes possible for us to better understand the gap between the good intentions of White adoptive parents (and most people) and the ways that race and racism still continue to negatively affect nearly all aspects of the lives of people of color, including adoptees of color.

Pointedly, understandings about race are carried within the language we use to talk about topics of interest. As Chris Weedon (1997) observes, "Language is the place where actual and possible forms of social organization and their likely social and political consequences are defined and contested" (20). We thus draw on the stories individuals from transracially adoptive families shared with us as a way to consider how racial knowledge influences how White adoptive parents raise their Black children.

Equality and Fair Treatment for All: A Language of Colorblindness and the Trouble with Not Seeing Color

Racial knowledge is a concrete and distinctive set of assumptions and characteristics about the nature and disposition of race and racism. Individuals use this set of assumptions as a type of interpretive lens for looking at the world of racial matters around them and understanding that racially organized world.

The interview excerpts at the start of the chapter illustrate how racial knowledge has guided the ways these adoptive parents have thought about and approached transracial adoption and the task of raising a Black child. Both Ms. March and Ms. White drew on assumptions that race matters are solely the concern of the individuals affected, not the concern of the group or collective. In that sense, they are blind to race. The individualistic lens through which these mothers looked at the race matters their adopted Black children experienced shielded them from the realization that Whites collectively do continue to maintain supremacy in nearly all domains of U.S. society, including employment, housing, health care, education, and more, while Blacks as a group continue to be systemically excluded from these same domains—the realization that this world is very much organized by color. The individualist lens filtered out the ways that race continues to significantly influence the lives and life chances of people of color.

As Whites using an individualist lens to make sense of racial matters, Ms. March and Ms. White are not alone. The individualist lens used by these adoptive mothers is based on the colorblind idea of equal-opportunity racism. *Equal-opportunity racism* is the idea that Whites are no longer the only ones who can be and sometimes are racist, since all things are now actually equal within our already supposedly equal society. Therefore, Blacks can now be just as racist, if not more racist, than Whites. Race doesn't apparently matter because everyone can be a racist.

In the excerpts, both Ms. March and Ms. White presume—as do many White people in the United States and globally (Coates 2007)—that racism and the potential to be racist are now universally and thus equally applicable to all individuals and social groups within the United States, including Whites and Blacks. The notion of reverse racism arises out of the assumption that because racial issues are now equally applicable to all, racism is now being turned around and used by people of color, the traditional targets of racism, against Whites, the traditional and original perpetrators of racism.

Put bluntly, this conception says that we are all, Black and White, equal now. Ms. March and Ms. White suggest that their adopted Black children have invoked the now-equal opportunity to enact racism by, respectively, being racist against Whites and hating all Whites. Ms. March and Ms. White likewise both indicate that they expect all individuals and groups to be treated fairly. They expect all to receive equal treatment, the equal application of a universal principle or standard for behavior. The two mothers are disappointed that their adopted children do not view others fairly. In these instances, it is White people who are not treating their Black children fairly or equally.

In particular, Ms. March's emphasis on equality as sameness, or equal and fair treatment across groups, is underscored as she reminds Darron that her family is not all White. Since the number of Whites and people of color are not equal in her home, Ms. March suggests that her Black daughter's apparent dislike of White people is unjustified and thus inappropriate. For her adopted daughter's racism against Whites to be potentially justified, the two groups, Whites and people of color, would have to be quantitatively equal in representation within the family, to achieve sameness across groups and thus give Whites the equal opportunity to respond back.

Ms. White's emphasis on equality of treatment likewise becomes especially visible as she reverses her adopted son's allegations of the negative behavior of Whites who "have taken so much" and thereby earned his apparent race-based hatred. Noting that a Black man could behave just as badly as her son alleges of White people, referring to "that pond-scum Black guy that did this," Ms. White highlights the importance of universal or equal application of any principle or expectation for behavior. For her son to be justified in saying a White man can be bad, then so too must he be willing to say a Black man can be just as bad. The possibility of being bad, according to Ms. White, must be applied equally for Whites *and* Blacks for her son to be justified in hating Whites.

Ms. White then provides an explanation and justification for her principle of equal application of behavior treatment by leveling the playing field between Whites and Blacks, saying "he knows too many wonderful White people." Put simply, racism goes both ways now. Blacks can now be just as bad and good as Whites can be. The number of "wonderful" Whites corrects the imbalance between bad Whites and Black people. We are all equal now.

Nearly all of the White adoptive parents we talked with expressed ideas that readily coincided with those of Ms. March and Ms. White. Most believed in the potential for equal-opportunity racism, the existence of reverse racism, and the necessity for fair treatment and equality among people of different racial backgrounds, including Whites and Blacks.

Ms. Ross, another adoptive mother, told us she was surprised to learn that Black people not only were able to turn racism back onto Whites—reverse racism—but would also turn racism against other Blacks. She explained, "The thing that's interesting to me is the racism that's among Blacks. You know that they have that [racism] among them." Racism used by Blacks against other Blacks, for Ms. Ross, meant that Black people were taking up the negative views about Blacks historically attributed to and used by Whites, and using these negative views against other Blacks.

Ms. Ross then proceeded to tell us the following story to illustrate racism used by Blacks against other Blacks. Laughing as she talked, Ms. Ross explained:

> We had this birth mom who stayed with us, and we stayed really good friends. She's the cutest Black girl. My other son had just had surgery, so I asked her to help us by flying out to pick up our [newly adopted Black] baby. She went and when she got there, she called me on the cell phone, and I said, "Yes?"
>
> Then she said, "I have to tell you something."
>
> I said, "What is it?"
>
> So she said, "This baby's not toasted, he's burnt."
>
> [laughing] Then I said, "Bring him on home, sister!"
>
> When she got here, we kind of talked about how they [Blacks] have that racism, the brown paper bag and, you know, all that kind of stuff. And I'm going, "You know, if you think Whites are prejudiced, that's pretty bad among Blacks too." I mean, I think that's ridiculous. I don't care.

At that point in the story, Mr. Ross had joined Ms. Ross in the conversation. He added, "We were told by her that the darker you are—you're expected to be of less value. You're not valued as much."

From the story recounted by Ms. Ross, we see the racist idea historically associated with Whites that being Black is a bad thing. But here it is being used by one Black person, the woman helping with the adoption in this case, against another Black, the Ross's adopted son. Interestingly, Ms. Ross, who as a White would be the one traditionally associated with the negative views about being Black, is not the one who cares about how dark-skinned her newly adopted son is. Instead, the adoption worker, someone who is Black, is the person who appears to have the negative views about Blacks.

The roles seem to be completely reversed as the adoption worker takes on the traditional White role of prejudice against Blacks and Ms. Ross, the White adoptive mother, takes on the traditional role of advocate for the Black community. Using the phrase "bring him on home, sister!" Ms. Ross suggests how far away she is from the traditional role of Whites: she knows her new son will be dark-skinned, but she still wants him to be brought home to her.

In sum, the story suggests that Blacks are now able to be as racist as Whites; we are all equal now. The White adoptive parents above, Ms. March, Ms. White, and Ms. Ross, draw on the idea of equality to show how being Black is basically the same as being White because race does not—and, more importantly, should not—matter. As a result, the traditional problems associated with racism and historically attributed to Whites, race-based prejudice and mistreatment, for example, can no longer be associated only with Whites because everyone, Black and White and every person of color, is now equal.

We should note here that we have a much different interpretation of the reported conversation. We believe the birth mother wanted to warn the adopting mother that the child was dark-skinned; she was trying to make sure that the adopting mother was OK with that because she was aware of the historical devaluing of Black skin.

Colorblindness: The Race Language and Metaphor for Contemporary Times

Equality is an idea that is a part of the language of everyday life and our history in U.S. society (Foner 1999). Most Americans have, and see themselves as adhering to, a strong sense of equality. As Zeus Leonardo (2009, 131) explains, "By and large, survey data suggest that white Americans indicate a belief in integration, disapproval with prejudicial attitudes, and support principles of equality among the races."

It is hardly surprising then that the White adoptive parents who participated in our study also expressed a strong sense of equality. Moreover, as with most White Americans, the sense of equality these adoptive parents expressed was anchored in colorblindness, that is to say, race neutrality, as if race does not and should not matter or be considered when interacting with others. As Leonardo (2009) notes, most White Americans publicly affirm that any type of racial preference is wrong. They believe, he argues, that the color of one's skin should not prevent access to opportunities in the forms of educational attainment, services, or goods.

Similarly, the White adoptive parents we interviewed said that it does not matter what color you are; whether you are "Black or White," like the lyrics to the Michael Jackson song suggest, everyone is essentially the same and requires the same treatment. The difference that difference makes, being Black, for example, is not considered legitimate within this notion of colorblind equality.

Leonardo (2009) could have been talking about the White adoptive parents in this study when he said, "This is not to suggest that fair-minded Americans do not recognize that racism continues into our present day and age. However, racism today is presumed to be more individualistic, not structural, and fundamentally attitudinal and multi-directional, not just white on black" (131). Put more crudely, race does not matter because everyone is equal and equality is colorblind—these are the racial understandings of colorblindness that are salient in our time.

The prominence and pervasiveness of the colorblind race language among White people in the United States is no small matter. Africans brought to this country, of course, were not free. Even the few Africans that came as indentured servants were not free in the sense Americans understand freedom today. Further, lynchings, deprivations, and brutality existed long after the end of slavery, and after the end of the Jim Crow era. While the civil-rights movement garnered substantial gains, great disparities in education and occupational opportunities remain. These distortions in the markets of freedom are the remains from slavery, Jim Crow, and the White privilege that continues to pervade American society. What scholars are now calling the "Colorblind era" (Leonardo 2009, 131) is hardly colorblind.

This language of colorblindness is a set of understandings, backed up by law and the courts, that "defines how people comprehend, rationalize, and act on race" (Lopez 2006, 6). These understandings of race combine to create a system of meaning about how to address and deal with race matters.

There are important and identifiable dimensions or contours that make up the language of colorblindness and serve as types of rules for how to handle race matters.

First, the language of colorblindness dictates that race should not be mentioned, seen, talked about, or taken seriously when (over)heard; the race rule is this: *see no race, speak no race, hear no race* (Leonardo 2009, 131). Within the language of colorblindness, the topic of race is taboo—unless you are going to mention how similar "they" (people of color) are to "us" (White people), or how much you (White people) love and celebrate "their" (people of color's) "exoticness" (differences from White people in hairstyles, clothing preferences, tastes in music, and more).

Second, the language of colorblindness requires a concerted focus on the individual, not the social group or collective as a whole. People are not to be seen as members of groups with specific collective experiences, accomplishments, and histories. All successes, and therefore and more importantly all failures, are deemed individual at best, and cultural at least. Given that equality within society, in terms of an equal playing field, is taken for granted as having already been accomplished, then the potential negative influence of unequal opportunities and resources no longer exists. Hence, group-based racism must always be downplayed, and racial progress must always be emphasized. Moreover, any existing evidence of racism must be seen as the exception rather than the rule, as incidents in isolation rather than part of a systemic pattern. Inequalities are to be defined as rapidly disappearing relics of the past that are about to be eradicated in line with the progressively increasing and expanding march toward racial equality.

Without the negative potential of unequal opportunities, then, all achievements and failures may rightfully be attributed to the individual. In the case of personal failures, for people of color, the group's culture may also be recognized as a negative contributing source. The ability of some groups and individuals to succeed despite their cultural backgrounds is viewed as evidence that the cultural backgrounds of some are more detrimental than those of others.

Third, because the individual is the focus, issues of race and racism must be seen as psychological and therefore intrapersonal. Race becomes individualized and therefore located within the individual person, and it is manifested as a study of attitudes, a project of making attitudinal changes within the psychology of how individuals think and talk—rather than their actual behavior or the patterned behavior of groups. Because any race-based negativity is viewed as psychological and as a holdover from the past, racist behavior and attitudes are to be understood as irrational and pathological, rather than as normal and as based on a person's vested interests.

The language of colorblindness thus has recognizable specific tenets about how to make sense of race. The assumptions put forth by the language of colorblindness position individuals to think about and act on race in particular ways, by serving as rules that regulate the boundaries of what is reasonable and unreasonable when trying to make sense of and act on racial matters. We have summarized these tenets of colorblindness, adapted from Leonardo (2009), in the following list:

1. Portray race as an individual process and thus a psychological matter of attitude and attitudinal changes. Portray racism as pathological and irrational, as largely occurring in isolation, and as exceptions to the rule, and not as a patterned activity.
2. Individualize successes and failures and any type of social disparity and inequality. Do not focus on group patterns. Suggest that if individuals work hard and have positive attitudes and motivation, then they will be successful despite any potential limitations of cultural background.
3. Emphasize racial progress and minimize racism as a thing of the very distant past—thus matters of genocide and slavery may not be considered. Downplay the role of institutions today in creating systemic race-based institutions. Focus on socioeconomic class, which also applies to Whites, *not race*, if systemic patterns have to be discussed.

Pointedly, the assumptions that characterize the language of colorblindness are significant because they combine to obscure the role of history and limit our awareness of the past and of patterns of race-based discrimination that continue to permeate and influence every aspect of every individual's life, both people of color and White people, albeit in different ways. Racial understandings are never neutral; they always have consequences, because individuals act on this knowledge and thus influence the world around them.

As represented by the excerpts at the beginning of this chapter, the White adoptive parents who participated in our study reflected the language of colorblind equality in their talk about race-based matters. The assumptions of colorblindness emerged through their emphasis on equal treatment of individuals and groups, regardless of color. By equalizing Whites and people of color, moreover, the collective experiences and histories of groups were erased and the historical racial domination perpetrated by Whites against people of color, Blacks in particular, was downplayed.

Race and racism were seen by these White adoptive parents as matters of attitudinal change—in this case, that their adopted Black children learn to have a better attitude toward White people and therefore strive for racial harmony to be achieved. The racial knowledge that White adoptive parents draw on, as we discuss further, does have consequences because it influences the ways they approach the task of interacting with and raising their Black and biracial children.

There are consequences for viewing race and racism as matters of individual psychology and thus minimizing the role of history and context. Understanding matters of racism as psychological matters, to be addressed by teaching individuals to tolerate and get along better with each other, obscures the continuity of race-based discrimination. The adoptees are not seen as members of a particular group with a particular collective history in which racial domination has been perpetrated collectively by Whites against them. As Leonardo (2009, 85) reminds us, "The sheer amount of [systemic] acts of violence or terror by whites toward racial minorities is overwhelming."

Failure to recognize and account for the White history of collective and systemic subjugation of Blacks allows Whites to be viewed as just one group among many groups within society, as if all groups have equal power to access society's resources and institutions. The historical, race-based structural oppression and subjugation of people of color in the United States has allowed Whites to create "a racialized social system that upholds, reifies, and reinforces the superiority of whites" (Leonardo 2009, 127). Manifestations of this race-based system of social structures privileging Whites are rendered visible by examining all major institutions within U.S. society. In our society, people of color consistently receive substandard and increasingly segregated forms of education, housing, and health care, among other things. Rates of unemployment, underemployment, and incarceration remain high. Access to income resources simultaneously remains low.

Importantly, the fact that people of color have *less* access to society's valued goods, resources, and opportunities necessarily means that Whites, by default, have *more* access to society's valued goods and opportunities. By applying the race-based assumptions of colorblindness, the historical role of White racial domination in securing and today maintaining a system of structures privileging Whites and White interests is obscured, because racial knowledge and race-based neutrality downplay institutional patterns and structures and systemic racial mistreatment. We cannot understand that there is no such thing as reverse racism when we use the language of colorblindness euphemistically to look at racial matters, consequently, because we cannot see that for reverse racism to exist, Blacks and other racial minorities would need to have the institutional ability and power equal to Whites to influence society's institutions and structures.

People of color still do not collectively hold the same institutional power as Whites to influence U.S. society's institutions and resources. This fact is immediately apparent when considering what group dominates and exercises control over the nation's media, big corporations, businesses, schools, politics, health care, housing, military, and police forces. As a group, Whites continue to maintain their superiority through structural domination by daily recreating and reinforcing patterns of activity, thinking, and talking that privilege their interests. The language of colorblindness helps to facilitate the continued structural domination of Whites by silencing any critiques of the systemic privileging of Whiteness and obscuring the visibility of Whites' collective power to control society's institutions and resources.

The language of colorblindness allows Whites to avoid recognizing how they daily benefit from a history of more than two hundred years of systemic policies, practices, and ideas that have collectively advantaged Whites at the expense of and off the backs of people of color. Colorblindness fosters a kind of racial amnesia among White people, allowing high-stakes benefits as a group whether individual Whites recognize these advantages or not. This distorted sense of a society as colorblind and now equal allows Whites to sleep peacefully at night while remaining largely ignorant of how the concept of race emerged in the first place.

A Brief History of How White People Became White and the Idea of Race Was Invented

Emerging approximately five hundred years ago, the modern or current concept of race is socially created when particular phenotypic differences (how people look physically) become associated with or linked to specific cognitive, moral, physical, and cultural characteristics as irreducible racial meanings applied to previously unclassified groups (Goldberg 1993; Wolfe 2002; West 2002; Omi and Winant 1994).

That the continent of Africa was exploited for labor and natural resources is well known. Perhaps less well known is the fact that the physical bodies of groups from various African regions, mainly the Western nations, were also explored as a social laboratory. The Europeans used the science of their day to experiment on and document the range of variability among human bodies and other living creatures. As Jean and John Comaroff (1993, 317) explain, "Vital bodily processes were widely held to depend upon outside stimuli—especially heat, a property dense with social and moral value. Africa's hot climate confirmed established European beliefs about the supposedly debauched condition of Africans, beliefs that were used continually to reinforce notions of racial superiority. 'Evidence' of these conditions was collected in the 'natural laboratory' along the frontier." Pointedly, the belief that Africans were socially, intellectually, physically, and in every other way backward signified that White people were superior. White superiority, in turn, gave rise to a number of assumptions about the origins of humankind and the inhumanity of Africans. The first Africans brought to the colonies were brought as indentured servants. As the experiment in capitalism continued, however, the period of indenturedness was extended. As the economy grew, racism expanded, and racist views dovetailed all too easily with enslavement.

The seemingly self-evident "fact" of Black inhumanity was well established in the eighteenth-century writings of François Bernier, who produced a racial typology that placed Europeans at the center of the human family. As Thomas Gossett (1997, 32) points out, "There are four general classifications of what would be called races—the Europeans, the Far Easterners, the 'Blacks,' and the Lapps." Gossett's analysis of eighteenth-century race science suggests that Blacks were placed at the bottom of a racial hierarchy, based on what Bernier described as "thick lips," "flat noses," and "hair like wool." Ideas about Black bodies later led to racist perceptions of flawed genes, a model for disease that contends Blacks have feeble DNA—which was then used to explain their greater susceptibility to bad health. Though these notions were construed early in European-African contact, they persisted through the slavery era and, in the minds of some people, through the civil-rights movement and even to current times.

Historically, according to Arthur Saint-Aubin (2002, 248), two specific scientific theories arose to account for physical differences between Whites and Blacks: environmentalism and biological determinism. Saint-Aubin notes that "Environmentalism postulated that racial characteristics such as skin color, hair texture, skull shape and size resulted from natural forces and conditions due to climate" (249). Adherents to these ideas believed that race was not fixed but could change given environmental circumstances, and that slavery was well suited for Blacks given their place on the evolutionary scale.

In contrast, biological determinism, as characterized by Saint-Aubin (2002, 249), "postulated that race was inborn resulting from what we now call genetics, and that race is immutable." Differences in skin tone, head shape, genitalia and hair texture between Blacks and Whites were thought to determine both behavior and moral constitution. As John Haller (1995, 9) notes, "the facial angle was the most extensively elaborated and artlessly abused criterion for racial somatology." Anglo-American and European science evoked specific discourse around the body and the status of humans (*Homo sapiens*), not only organizing them in terms of genera and species but racializing the differences in physiognomy. Bodies, skulls, facial angles, eye shape, and other factors not consistent with Northern European features of blonde hair and blue eyes, for example, were thought to characterize a subspecies of *Homo sapiens*. The physical features of racial difference purportedly determined and predicted behavior that science was committed to proving.

Ritchie Witzig (1996) postulates that the European scientists Carl Linnaeus and especially his student, Johann Blumenbach, created the subclassifications of our genus and species and ranked them accordingly to invented pseudoscientific racial theories of mankind. Blumenbach deemed his own people living in the Caucasus Mountains of Europe to be the most beautiful people (Diamond 1994). He ranked African on the low end of their taxonomy scale. Thus Blackness, as defined by Linnaeus and Blumenbach, described one who was crafty but indolent, negligent, and governed by caprice. These were terms that would later serve as representations for Black culture.

Stephen Jay Gould (1999) writes extensively about racial theories and procedures carried out on the African body, experiments that would seemingly underscore the racial inferiority and perpetual "otherness" of Blacks. Gould notes that some authors' use of Darwin's ideas suggested that non-Whites were stuck in an evolutionary holding pattern that made them more childlike in nature and caused Blackness. Accordingly, the physical differences in Blacks that were perceived to predetermine mortality, morbidity, and poverty were now self-evident as documented through scientific study. Not only did the measuring of skulls, heads, genitalia, and other anatomical markers marginalize Blacks in the mind of Western science, but these practices also became the signifiers of irreducible difference—ways of producing an epistemology of innate difference between Whites and Blacks. Black phenotypes were not merely observed, but rather, for Europeans, they "clarified" that the Africans' culture and habits made them considerably "less than" Whites—subhuman.

North American Blacks were thus reduced to the sum of their parts. The body parts of African Americans, in turn, were deemed to determine personality and intelligence. As we have noted, many of these same assumptions about Blacks persist, though not always in explicitly biological terms. The idea that Blacks are poor today because they do not have the will to work hard, for example, is commonly viewed as a cultural rather than biological effect within contemporary racial parlance.

Historian Winthrop D. Jordan (1974, 6) writes about the first contact as the fulcrum of the racializing processes, "For Englishmen, the most arresting characteristic of the newly discovered African was his color." He mentions that few European travelers failed to comment on the Blackness of Africans, which was important in constructing them as abnormal. Prior to New World ventures, no other color conveyed so much emotional impact. According to Jordan, the *Oxford English Dictionary*, before the sixteenth century, included "*Black* as foul, atrocious, horrible, wicked, sinister and baneful to name a few negative denotations" (33). In addition, there were biblical ideas connected to the color black denoting it as a curse; so when the English encountered Africans, they had a familiarity with blackness that essentially primed them to view Africans in a disapproving light. Africans represented a different kind of human being, a being that Europeans were only accustomed to in the popular stories and writings of the day.

Consequently, European contact resulted in the exclusion of Africans. Further, concepts of racialization made European notions of progress and Enlightenment tenets possible. These conceptions of enlightenment (as they were applied to Africans) were brought to the United States. These schemas enabled the dominant ideologies of the Enlightenment era to function. The negative representations of non-White peoples were important; they allowed Europeans and the new Americans to disqualify Africans and African Americans from the human family. Ironically, the complexities worked within a nation that claimed the abstract democratic principles of a romanticized Greek and Roman heritage. Accordingly, universal humanism required "[t]he racialism of the West, slavery, imperialism, the destruction of indigenous cultures" (Kelley 1997, 106). Slavery, in particular, provided the economic base for bourgeois democratic revolution in the West (Kelley 1997). As Charles Mills (1997, 27) states it, "European humanism usually meant that only Europeans were human." White bodies, as the apotheosis of humanness, were privileged and reified in the history and evolution of race.

We see the continued privileging of White bodies and Whiteness recreated and maintained today through what has been referred to as *the White problem*, as we explain further in the next section.

The White Problem: Considering the Consequences of White Racial Knowledge

White people, as we have seen, thus have produced racial knowledge—a certain kind of knowledge usually expressed and communicated today through the language of colorblindness. This White racial knowledge is derived from history and developed over time, as we have also seen. White racial knowledge is important because it serves as a basis on which individuals make choices about, understand, and act on the world around them.

Hence, Whites are participants in racial matters who actively engage in negotiating race; White people are not unknowing bystanders who know nothing about race, and, as illustrated, the racial knowledge White people most oftentimes draw on is the language of colorblind equality. How and where do White people acquire the knowledge they have about race?

As Ellis Cose (1997, 193) has observed,

> The perception gap quietly shapes how Blacks and Whites interpret the world, their experiences and each other. It shows up in our assumptions and rationalizations, in our decisions and politics, in our neighborhoods and schools. To be sure, not all Whites think alike about race, nor do all Blacks. But the consensus within each race is striking.

It is not, moreover, coincidental that there are similarities within the ways White people make sense of race-based matters.

The similarities in the ways Whites talk about and enact racial matters emerge because they are derived from cultural assumptions that reflect a social group's patterned ways of thinking. Individuals, as they grow up and are socialized into the group's social organization, learn how to draw from particular group-based patterns and habits of thinking, acting, knowing, and understanding the self in relationship to the group. The evidence of White racial understandings is well reflected in the recent CNN pilot study conducted by University of Chicago professor Margaret Beale Spencer. Spencer's study reveals that "white children had an overwhelming bias toward white, and black children also had a bias toward white, but it was not nearly as strong as the bias shown by the white children" ("Readers" 2010). This study suggests that Whiteness is saturated and well established within U.S. society to such an extent that even people of color are impacted. Consequently, there is a difference between White people's racial knowledge and White racial knowledge.

What are the consequences of White racial knowledge, then? How does it influence the ways individuals understand and make decisions about the world? The answer is best illustrated by the example of *the White problem* (Bennett 1972; DuBois 1940/1968; Wright 1957), a concept derived from the Black radical tradition (Dawson 1994; Olson 2004). In response to a reporter's question about race relations in the United States, Richard Wright (1946, cited in Kinnamon and Fabre 1993, 99) famously explained, "There isn't any Negro problem; there is only a white problem." Redefining U.S. society's race *problem* as White instead of Black, "Wright called attention to its hidden assumptions—that racial polarization comes from the existence of blacks rather than the behavior of whites, that black people are a 'problem' for whites rather than fellow citizens entitled to justice, and that, unless otherwise specified, 'American' means 'white'"(Lipsitz 2006, 1).

The racial assumptions identified by Wright are significant because they represent what at one time in history were conventional ideas, beliefs, and understandings about race and equality collectively shared by Whites. Both individually and collectively, Whites used this racial knowledge, that is to say, these underlying ideas, beliefs, and assumptions, to interpret and justify everyday matters regarding equality and race. Clearly, "[i]t was a stroke of genius really for white Americans to give Negro Americans the name of their problem, thereby focusing attention on symptoms (the Negro and the Negro community) instead of causes (the white man and the white community)" (Bennett 1972, 1).

White racial knowledge is therefore a concrete body of race-based understandings that Whites created and continue to draw on. Transforming to adapt to shifting historical conditions, White racial knowledge functions as the hidden referent that privileges the interests, values, experiences, and beliefs of Whites and the superiority of Whiteness. Privileging characteristics associated with Whites with a status of normalcy and the state of being human, White racial knowledge is a way of knowing and being in the world that provides Whites with an identity and a corresponding sense of belonging and entitlement.

Evaluated against Whites, people of color are then racially marked as interlopers, the denigrated others who do not belong, while Whites are positioned as rightfully in control of society's institutions and resources. "To be an 'All-American' means, by definition, *not* to be an Asian American, Pacific-

American, American Indian, Latino, Arab-American or African-American" (Marable 1993, 113; emphasis in the original). As the dominant group in control of the institutions that generate and police cultural meanings, Whites have historically used their position of dominance to impose their perspectives on society as *the* viewpoint, and *the* right way to understand that which is needed to be fully human (Douglass 1852/1972; Feagin 2006; Wise 2009).

This systemic privileging of interests, values, beliefs, histories, and experiences associated with White people has allowed Whites to view themselves and their racial knowledge as normal, while everyone else is exotic, ethnic, and otherwise the racial other. Learning to privilege Whiteness begins very early among Whites, as noted by one scholar: "[F]or white people, [race] is about everyone else. While having black skin or almond shaped eyes or coarse and curly hair are clearly signs of 'difference' according to mainstream culture, having yellow hair or green eyes or white skin are often not viewed in this way by the people who possess them. That is because it is always whiteness that is centered and assumed" (Rothenberg 2002, 2).

Accordingly, White racial knowledge is at the center of processes of race-based domination. Following Leonardo (2009, 75), we define *racial domination* as "those acts, decisions, and policies that white subjects perpetrate on people of color." White racial domination happens, importantly, not behind the backs of White people or through random acts of race hatred committed by individuals. As a group and individually, Whites daily "take resources from people of color all over the world, appropriate their labor, and construct policies that deny minorities' full participation in society" (Leonardo 2009, 76). Drawing on White racial knowledge, Whites actively re-create and secure supremacy in almost all facets of social life through processes of racial domination (Bonilla-Silva, 2003).

Being White, however, doesn't automatically signify the use of White racial knowledge "although there certainly is a preponderance of white people who interpret social life through white racial knowledge" (Leonardo 2009, 109). As Leonardo (2009, 109) notes, "white people's racial knowledge is not synonymous with white racial knowledge."

Indeed, being White and Whiteness as racial knowledge are less about skin color and more about how individuals interpret and make decisions about the surrounding context. People of color may espouse or embody White racial knowledge. As oftentimes happens with individual White people who do antiracist work and learn to acknowledge their White privilege and denounce White racism, Whites may likewise learn to appropriate the racial knowledge generated from the historical experiences of people of color.

Language, Cognitive Frames, and Inequality: Learning White Racial Knowledge

As we have noted, White racial knowledge is carried within and reflected by the language individuals use to talk about topics of interest. As individuals talk, they use language to frame the topic they are talking about. Language, made up of both implicit and explicit beliefs, images, understandings, and assumptions carried within talk, frames topics of concern by providing sets of cognitive meaning systems or interpretive lenses that guide the ways individuals make sense of what they see and do (Foucault 1970, 1972; Franklin 1999; Popkewitz and Brennan 1998; Rose 1989).

As illustrated by *the White problem*, framing particular topics in specific ways becomes habitual and is group based. Individuals, as a member of a particular social group, learn from a young age how to frame specific topics in specific, collectively held, and culturally sanctioned ways. Frames facilitate learning and social understanding by filtering new information and experiences from daily life into the person's existing understandings of how to act and think (Bhabha 1989; Bonilla-Silva 2003; Scott 1992; Weedon 1997, 1999).

Pointedly, frames can also be oppressive and destructive (Thompson and Tyagi 1996; Yancey 2004). By filtering out ideas and information that challenge false, distorted, or stereotypical ideas about racial minorities, frames help to reinforce and recreate patterns of systemic racism. Frames bridge and make concrete patterns of systemic racism in the daily lives of individuals as they apply group-based, patterned ways of reasoning that justify inequities and filter out counterperspectives (Jordan and Weedon 1995; Kluegel and Smith 1986; Krysan and Lewis 2004; Roediger 1999, 2002; Sears et al. 2000).

The White Racial Frame: A Theoretical Tool for Making Sense of Race Matters

To help us better understand matters of transracial adoption and White racial knowledge, we turn to Leslie Picca and Joe Feagin's (2007; Feagin 2010b) notion of the White racial frame. This theoretical tool provides a useful way of understanding how White adoptive parents acquire knowledge about race and then convey these understandings to their children. The White racial frame also helps us understand how individuals of goodwill may and often do support and affirm racist oppression by embodying and furthering "white-supremacist values and beliefs even though they may not embrace racism as prejudice or domination (especially domination that involves coercive control)" (hooks 1989, 113).

It is our perspective that, for the most part, people do not wish to do harm to others, especially not based on race. Yet, as we have seen through our discussion of transracial adoption and race in the United States to this point, race and racism nevertheless continue to be major factors negatively structuring the lives of people of color in our society. If we can better understand how people of goodwill and helpful intentions may unwittingly participate in perpetuating negative race-based outcomes for people of color, it becomes possible for all of us to begin working together to bridge that historical gap that remains in our nation between our democratic ideals of equality and the systemic racism that still plagues our society. Ironically, racism is most of the time perpetuated by the nice, well-intentioned, good people of society, not the hateful extremists that most of us tend to think about when we think about racism in our country. Racism is likewise not necessarily perpetrated by the old, the uneducated, and the working-class Whites in society.

For transracial adoption, the potential for Whites of goodwill to be unwittingly involved in furthering racism is a critical topic to examine, as those involved in adopting across racial lines are most often individuals who have altruistic aims and do not wish to harm anyone, particularly not their own children.

Passed down over generations as habitual ways of thinking, the White racial frame refers to "an organized set of racialized ideas, stereotypes, emotions, and inclinations to discriminate" (Feagin 2006, 25). Five important dimensions make up the White racial frame: (1) assumptions about the overall superiority of Whites in culture, achievement, and morality as justification for White control and dominance of institutions, and beliefs that people of color are inferior and less significant in the making and maintaining of U.S. society; (2) negative stereotypes about people of color; (3) emotions racialized by association with racial assumptions in the form of negative stereotypes; (4) recurring individual and group enactments of racialized knowledge; and (5) the larger institutional structures in which racialized performances are enacted (Feagin 2006; Picca and Feagin 2007).

During the interviews we conducted, there were many times that the White adoptive parents conveyed stories that illustrated a White racial framing of the incidents being recounted. Describing an example of how she and her husband worked to bring the culture of their Black son into the life of their family, Ms. West recalled:

> There was this Black social worker around here, and we had met with her many times. She told us about this place. And the first time [Mr. West] and I went, when he pulled up outside, I said, "I'm not going in there." I mean, there were bars on the windows, in the wrong part of town. And he said, "Where's the girl I married? Where's your adventure?" And I went, "Okay, all right." She was the best cook ever. . . . All of the basketball players [from the local professional team] eat there all the time. We even ate Christmas dinner down there once with the whole family.

Ms. West's account of going to eat at a restaurant located on the wrong side of town manifests several dimensions of White racial framing. The visual image of Blackness is created through the association of a restaurant recommended to Mr. and Ms. West by a Black woman. That the restaurant caters to a Black clientele and serves cuisine associated with Blacks is established by the distinctiveness and exoticism of this journey to this particular restaurant (otherwise Ms. West might not have mentioned the trip) and the link to basketball players who are in this case presumed to be Black.

In turn, the restaurant's characteristics of "bars on the windows" and being located in the "wrong part of town" draw on negative stereotypes and cultural biases that associate Blackness with a space of danger, violence, and other forms of social deviance and pathology. Ms. West's reaction of fear in response to her arrival at the restaurant underscores the connection between Blackness and danger. Mr. West's own sense of adventure, implied by his query about where his wife's sense of adventure was, then not only reinforces this sense of danger and violence associated with Blackness—you need a sense of adventure and courage to go into dangerous areas—but also serves to frame him and his wife in a strongly positive and active role as brave and good people for knowingly volunteering to adventure over into a place that they are aware is potentially dangerous and violent, and therefore bad.

The aspects of the White racial frame are highlighted in the excerpted interview by the distinctiveness of Blackness as bad, and Whiteness as brave and courageous. It is proferred as if White people venturing over into a Black space are daring pioneers going where few White people have gone before. The moral superiority of Whiteness is achieved through the victory of good over bad, as Ms. West draws on her sense of adventure and not only goes into a Black restaurant and presumptively bad space but then amplifies this accomplishment of good over bad by enjoying the meal enough to return for repeated visits. The triumph of White people crossing into a dangerous Black space is expressed in the account of the Wests returning to the Black restaurant with the entire family for Christmas dinner, a meal that is often taken to symbolize the ultimate in family bonding, unity, love, and harmony. The association of parent as protector of vulnerable offspring illustrates the height of this moral victory of the White adoptive parents crossing into a Black urban setting, because ideally good parents would not bring their children into dangerous locations, especially not on purpose.

The emotions manifested through the fear of association with a Black space and the feelings of achieving enough comfort in a Black place to return are revealing of the White racial-framing process. That White people can choose whether or not to cross over into a Black space likewise reflects the sociohistorical context, in which White racial domination has enabled Whites collectively to have freedom of mobility. People of color do not typically have choices as to whether or not they will cross over into White spaces, and most certainly they do not determine the terms on which they must negotiate and interact with others within those White spaces.

The restaurant trip reflects, then, both the power of Whiteness to facilitate Whites' mobility across social spaces and the terms of their interactions within those social spaces. In the interview, Ms. West acknowledged that it was a "soul food" restaurant. The cuisine of the restaurant recommended by the Black social worker was celebrated as different from the kind of fare typically available to the family, thus underscoring how normal the characteristics of Whiteness are within U.S. society. Crossing over into the Black space of the restaurant reflects a White racial framing that highlights the goodness and superiority of Whites in having accomplished the ultimate in not only crossing over into the danger of Blackness but then also going above and beyond by becoming comfortable in Blackness, enjoying themselves, and then returning to do it again, this time with their family—a victory indeed for these pioneers of race, since we know from the tremendous amount of scholarship on White racial attitudes that White people in the United States overwhelmingly live in segregated areas with little contact with people of color, especially any contact that involves equal status and friendship beyond the acquaintance level (Jackman 1994).

The conceptualization of Whites as morally superior—the idea that White people are brave and courageous and Blacks morally inferior—and the assumption that Black people are dangerous and violent are not new: they can be traced back to the first contact between Whites and Blacks. Notably, the assumptions of White superiority and Black inferiority are not necessarily consciously or intentionally drawn on during the recounting of the story. Nor does the use of assumptions of White superiority and Black inferiority necessarily involve any type of race hate or negativity, as illustrated. Nor does it suggest that White adoptive parents do not love their Black children.

For the richness of the restaurant trip to be fully tapped into, however, the assumptions of White superiority and Black inferiority would have to be investigated. The material conditions that shape and influence Black spaces would have to be accounted for—fewer available jobs, for example, race-based discrimination exhibited consistently in hiring practices, and more. The White racial frame is more than a deeply embedded cognitive tool historically used by Whites; as we have seen in the present discussion and in other examples in this book, it is a collectively shared perspective that guides the thinking of White people and their interactions with people of color. Because the White racial frame is a historically produced and embedded process of thinking and acting, individual White people like Mr. and Ms. West draw on but did not invent the racial knowledge they use to make sense of race encounters. As we have stated, individuals from all groups are socialized into the ways of thinking and acting that are particular to their group. Accordingly, it is not appropriate to blame individuals for systems of thinking and acting that are historical and thus precede them.

The White racial frame has been developing for more than five hundred years. It is therefore ridiculous to suggest that particular White people today are responsible for the White racial framing they are likely to employ to navigate the world. Moreover, and as we have argued repeatedly, White people, like everyone else, are thinking and acting subjects who make choices. White people make choices about the White racial frame, then, although not always immediately, consciously, or explicitly. At the same time, not all five dimensions of the White racial frame will be evident within every interaction or speech act enacted by individuals who are White.

Summary

The White adoptive parents we worked with as a part of this book's study were the most amazing and loving people, who opened up their hearts, homes, and lives to us. In no way would we like to suggest that these individuals and families are anything but what they are—incredibly wonderful people who, like us, are not perfect and do not know everything. Our point then is not toward criticism or blame of the White adoptive parents and adoptees in this study, White people in general, or anyone else for that matter.

What we hope to do instead is show how and why the race-based systems of inequality that all of us today were born into are oftentimes being recreated and perpetuated despite the good intentions and love of very sincere people. Our hope is that by identifying these moments where White racial knowledge is applied and historical patterns of racism are reestablished, we can help create a situation where all vested individuals can come together to create a more democratic society and world. It is our hope that what we have learned from the ways White racial knowledge operates can help all of us work together to struggle against racism, a historical system that continues to destroy too many lives and families.

Because White adoptive parents, like the ones we worked with, are often good people who really do want to make the world a better, more democratic, and socially just place, we hope that by exploring the ways White racial knowledge influences individuals and their actions within the context of transracial adoption, we can all learn how to make the world a better place for now and the future. By understanding how White racial knowledge positions individuals to see and act on the world in particular ways, it becomes possible to begin moving away from blaming White adoptive parents and other White people and their attitudes in particular for the race-based inequities in society. Individuals' racial understandings are symptoms, not causes, of inequities in education. As we learn more about the functions and consequences of White racial knowledge in structuring the distribution of resources in society, we may become better equipped to interrupt processes of race-based dominance and begin to learn how to make racial equality a true reality.

CHAPTER FOUR

Research on Transracial Adoption

What Do We Know?

So we got a call from [an adoption agency] saying they had a biracial child for us. We thought about it and thought about what we would want to do, and we talked to our parents and asked them how they felt. Both sets of parents said that they would prefer if we'd just wait for another child that matched.

—Ms. Davis, White adoptive parent

He'd come home from school when he was young and say, "Mom, the kids at school were calling me black. I'm not black, I'm brown." So we went through that.

—Ms. Hansen, White adoptive parent

I think that's [Whites being unaware of the ongoing realities of racism] one of my biggest frustrations, because I'm aware of well-meaning White folks, and I don't like that, because we are very aware, especially because of my profession. We don't want to just give it superficial treatment, and yet I recognize that we don't have some of the insight or information. The best that we do . . . is just try to not to make it a big issue.

—Mr. Vest, White adoptive parent

BEING DIFFERENT is a profoundly significant matter among human beings. What to do with differences can cause consternation, suffering, and grief among us *Homo sapiens* because we have fixated on insignificant factors like race, gender, class, religion, and ableness. Power is at the root of inequalities within a capitalistic society such as the United States. The history of race, as demonstrated in this book, has determined, to a large extent, our national fixation on profit-driven motives at the expense of our inherent moral worth.

At an intellectual level, all of us know what to do with differences. It's easy—we simply treat those who are different from ourselves with the same dignity and respect that we want to be treated with, and that we deserve as fellow human beings. Yet, if it's so easy, then why don't we do it? Looking at our historical track record it is readily apparent that we have continued to inflict a great deal of indignity and harm on each other sheerly on the basis of differences among us. Audre Lorde (1984, 115) explains,

> Institutionalized rejection of difference is an absolute necessity in a profit economy which needs outsiders as surplus people. As members of such an economy [and world], we have *all* been programmed to respond to the human differences among us with fear and loathing and to handle that difference in one of three ways: ignore it, and if that is not possible, copy it if we think it is dominant, or destroy it if we think it is subordinate. But we have no patterns for relating across our human differences as equals.

The belief that some forms of difference are superior to others has historically authorized the right of some to dominate those marked as "other." In the United States historically, physical differences served to sanction the White enslavement, subjugation, and domination of African-descent peoples as chattel property—the foundation of today's society and of the race-based disparities we see currently between Blacks and Whites.

Differences likewise remain today at the center of transracial adoption (TRA),[1] differences in race emerging out of historical relations between Whites and people of color. Transracial adoption would not exist without a focus on racial differences. Not surprisingly, then, transracial adoption "is considered the most visible of all forms of adoption because the physical differences between adoptive parents and adoptee are more apparent and immutable" (Lee 2003, 712).

The epigraphs at the opening of this chapter are representative of the pervasiveness of the differences that differences make in the lives of transracially adopted children and youth and their families. At some level and at some point in time, all White adoptive parents must face and decide how to address issues of racial differences between themselves and their children of color. We are not the only researchers who have examined transracial adoption and race. Other research, which we review in this chapter, has found that when White parents solely declare that "love is enough," the children suffer needlessly because racial differences are not adequately addressed. The extant body of research on transracial adoption serves as a backdrop to the challenges and opportunities faced by the transracially adoptive families. Throughout this chapter, we use excerpts from the interviews with the transracial families. We use these as a springboard to explore and discuss in more detail similar yet different findings in the work of other researchers.

Given the rapidly growing numbers of transracially adoptive families, it is especially important that we review and make sense of the patterns emerging from what we already know and do not yet know or understand about transracial adoption. Three types of studies have emerged from research conducted on transracial adoption since the 1970s: (1) studies that have examined children's overall adjustment to transracial adoption, covering self-esteem issues, school achievement, and levels and types of adjustment problems; (2) studies that have explored the racial-identity development of adoptees; and (3) studies that have identified and examined the cultural-socialization practices and outcomes of White adoptive parents teaching children of color how to cope with race and racism.

We begin by looking at the outcomes of studies that were published in the early years of scholarship. We then consider the racial-identity studies by comparing the findings on Black adoptees with the studies of identity development of people of color. We conclude the chapter by examining more recent explorations of how White parents prepare their adoptive children to address race-based mistreatment. We compare their experiences with how Black parents teach their children about race.

Research on Adjusting to Transracial Adoption

The majority of early empirical works on transracial adoption evaluated outcomes for TRAs on IQ, school success, self-esteem, and a variety of other traditional measures of achievement. These measures, however, fail to take into account the grinding, sometimes abrasive effects that race relations cause in the United States. White adoptive parents are often unaware of how race impacts and shapes the daily experiences of their adopted children, and they must learn of this vicariously. If we can understand how White adoptive parents think about race and how that thinking affects adoptees, we can begin to understand the identity issues that adoptees of color struggle with. Further, we can then begin to understand how White parents come to understand race through their adoptees' experience.

Researchers in the 1970s and 1980s (e.g., Alstein and Simon 1977; Simon and Alstein 1987) published scholarship that argued that Black adoptees in White homes were no more at risk of psychological harm than same-race adoptees. Lucille Grow and Deborah Shapiro (1974) studied the success of TRAs through personal interviews with parents, siblings, and teachers and administered personality tests to Black adoptees, comparing their test scores with those of same-race adopted children. The authors determined that 77 percent of the children adjusted well in White homes—in terms of self-esteem, academic achievement, and level of adjustment problems. For them, this was conclusive evidence that TRA was successful in finding permanent homes for Black children. Likewise, Penny Johnson and colleagues (1987) found that when Black adoptees living in White communities had little contact with other Black Americans, three fourths of them seemed well adjusted and comfortable in their environment. Other analysts found that Black adoptees in predominately White communities had higher IQ scores than those adopted by same-race families (Moore 1987; Scarr et al. 1993). These studies comprise diverse empirical works and form a basis of support for race-neutral family-placement practices.

Other researchers, however, argue that "[t]he body of research examining African-American transracial adoptees is very limited and consists primarily of studies conducted over 20 years ago" (Smith et al. 2008, 21). Most "used very small sample sizes and assessed children at young ages, and some did not have comparison groups of children placed in same-race families" (21). In response to early studies in the field, more recent studies on transracial adoption have attempted to employ more rigorous research methods by using multivariate analyses to identify influences and factors structuring child outcomes. (See, for example, Brooks and Barth 1999; Feigelman 2000.) Similarly, other TRA studies conducted since 1990 have refined constructs used to measure racial-identity development, sense of group orientation, and methods of socialization (Brooks 2001; De Haymes and Simon 2003; Juffer 2006).

Richard Lee (2003) argues that there are three main types among the recent studies: expanded outcomes studies, racial-identity studies, and cultural-socialization studies. Lee also notes that for many researchers, the underlying assumption was that transracial adoption would not pose problems for adoptees of color if there were no significant group differences on psychological-adjustment measures. Early studies did not consider the racial incidents and experiences encountered by adoptees to analyze how these race-specific encounters may have influenced psychological adjustment. The more recent studies suggest that while TRA in itself does not produce psychological problems or social maladjustment challenges for adoptees, there are significant dimensions of the transracial-adoption experience that may combine to cause serious adversities for adoptees and sometimes for their adoptive families (Smith et al. 2008).

In sum, the TRA studies conducted since the early 1990s provide a more nuanced, complex, and composite view of the possibilities and challenges generated by interracial family-placement practices. In general, three main conclusions can be drawn from the studies of TRA and the racial-socialization practices of Black parents. First, transracial adoption itself is not necessarily a challenge for adoptees and does not necessarily have to create challenges for them. However, given the ongoing pervasiveness of racism, transracially adopted children often do experience a range of challenges derived from the combination of factors related to the historical and current issues of race in the United States. Second, because of the challenges associated with being racially different within an overwhelmingly White world, the critical role of parents in raising children is amplified within the context of transracial adoption. The ways in which White adoptive parents handle the race-related risks associated with TRAs can facilitate or hinder the positive development of identity and self-esteem, and the overall well-being of adoptees. Third, White adoptive parents who explicitly address their adopted children's race-related needs are more likely to foster the development of the child's fullest potential. Discussing race with children is found to be a very important activity, according to studies on educational television and parent-child discussion on racial attitudes. When children discuss with their parents issues of race and racism after watching educational television shows like *Little Bill* and *Sesame Street*, for example, they value difference more than if they watch these shows without parental involvement (Vittrup 2009). Parents provide a context for simple racial themes that play out in educational television that children may not be able to decipher. Toward this end, children fare better overall and develop healthier identities when parents take the time to talk with them about racial differences rather than ignoring, minimizing, or downplaying vital racial issues.

Three of the most significant dimensions of TRA correlated with negative outcomes for adoptees of color include (1) perceptions of being different, (2) struggles associated with fitting into a family and community, and (3) adjustment problems that derive from struggles over trying to fit in socially. For many transracially adopted children, feeling and being looked at as racially different is a significant and daily challenge (Brooks and Barth 1999; Clemetson and Nixon 2006; Feigelman 2000). Skin color has been identified as a major factor contributing to adoptees' feelings of being "different" (Keith and Herring 1991; McRoy and Grape 1999). Indeed, some White adoptive parents reported that their children, particularly those with darker skin color, expressed a desire to be White (Juffer 2006). We found, during interviews, that many of the Black adoptees from our study clearly identified with the White and Asian students while in high school.

Of her own experiences as an international Vietnamese adoptee, Indigo Williams Willing (2004, 650) writes, "Once I began school, I continued to try to fit in with my predominantly white peers, hoping to pass as one of them even though, to my distress, I was regularly referred to as 'the Asian girl.'" For many adoptees, the sense of being racially different creates a struggle to fit into their adoptive White families and the surrounding communities in which they live. Pointedly, the struggle to fit in often becomes more intense as adoptees begin to have experiences outside of the home—at school, and within the larger community (Tatum 2004; Twine 1997). Dating emerges in TRA-outcome studies as a particularly salient occasion for the struggle to fit in (Clemetson and Nixon 2006; Mohanty et al. 2006). We discuss this further in subsequent chapters.

The struggle to find a social place within the family and community often puts adoptees of color at risk for adjustment problems (Smith et al. 2008). In particular, transracially adopted African American male youths are twice as likely to exhibit adjustment problems. Manifestations of these adjustment problems include reports of disruptive behavior at school, negative encounters with law-enforcement officials, and other serious social offences (DeBerry et al. 1996; De Haymes and Simon 2003; Feigelman 2000; Weinberg et al. 2004).

Racial-Identity Studies on Transracial Adoption

Racial-identity studies form a second type of recent research on TRA. According to Ruth McRoy (1989, 66), "Racial group identity refers to one's self-perception and sense of belonging to a particular group. It includes not only how one describes and defines oneself, but also how one distinguishes oneself from members of other ethnic groups and the extent to which an individual has acquired behaviors specific to the particular racial groups." Within the purview of identity development, Black children slowly gain an understanding of racial labels and emotional responses and attempt to make sense of what it means to be Black in a White society. Racial-identity development is thus a profoundly important process for children of color because it connects them to a community full of received wisdom from past generations about successfully coping with racism and discrimination.

Significantly, African Americans with well-developed, positive racial identities have been found to have high self-esteem and overall better psychological health and well-being, coping skills, and resilience against racism (Cross et al. 1991; Poindexter-Cameron and Robinson 1997; Spencer 1988). In contrast, African Americans with less developed racial identities "have been found to be associated with low levels of self-actualization and self-acceptance, high feelings of anxiety, inferiority, personal inadequacy, hypersensitivity, memory impairment, paranoia, hallucinations, alcohol concerns, and general psychological distress" (Thompson et al. 2000, 199). Blacks with low levels of racial identity are likewise at more risk for marital discord, academic difficulties in school, and low self-esteem (Anderson 1991; Carter 1995; Parham and Helms 1981; Speight et al. 1996). In sum, the literature on Black self-identity shows a number of concerns. Some of these concerns are extremely important, but they have not been examined extensively in most of the studies on transracial adoption.

To develop a racial identity, transracially adopted children must find ways to negotiate and adapt to a racially conscious society, sometimes without adequate parental and sibling models. The more recent research in the Black community has used reliable and valid measures of racial/ethnic identity (Frasch and Brooks 2003; Hollingsworth 1997; Lee 2003). The recent research documents the ways racial identity is structured by both the race experiences and adjustment outcomes in the life of an adoptee (Anderson 1991; Poindexter-Cameron and Robinson 1997). Put simply, race experiences directly influence the racial-identity development of TRAs. Recent research, therefore, explores the effects of transracial adoption on adoptees' sense of racial pride and comfort with their racial group of origin.

At the same time, transracial adoptees have a wide range of experiences. As a result, they vary in the way they negotiate and adapt to race, and the way they incorporate race into a personal identity (Phinney 1989; Thompson et al. 2000; Yoon 2001). As Lee (2003, 719) states, "[G]reater awareness of prejudice and discrimination during adolescence and adulthood may lead TRAs to experience a range of conflicting emotions regarding race and ethnicity." These emotions can include denial, shame, pride, discomfort, and other reactions. Often reflecting conflicting emotions, the adoptees' experiences of engaging race and racism contribute to the ways they perceive themselves and their role, status, and opportunities within the family and larger society (Hollingsworth 1997; Kallgren and Caudill 1993).

Traditionally, measures of racial identity have been assessed by examining the extent to which adoptees use racial self-descriptors (DeBerry et al. 1996; Hollingsworth 1997; Simon and Alstein 2000). When adoptees express high levels of race dissonance, for example expressing a preference for White dolls over dolls reflecting their own skin tones, they have been identified as having lower levels of racial-identity development (Rotheram and Phinney 1987; Freundlich and Lieberthal 2000; Huh and Reid 2000; McRoy 1994; Simon and Alstein 2000). While many TRAs report describing themselves as White, mainly to identify with their adoptive parents' racial background during their formative years, as adults they identify with their community of origin and describe themselves (correctly) as people of color (Baden 2002; Freundlich and Lieberthal 2000; Westhues and Cohen 1998). Age, emotional and social development, and awareness of prejudice appear to influence the race preferences and racial-identity development of TRAs (DeBerry et al. 1996; Simon and Alstein 2000).

At the same time, racial and ethnic identity appears to emerge in a weaker form among TRAs raised in predominately White communities (Cederblad et al. 1999; DeBerry et al. 1996). Leslie Hollingsworth (1997) conducted a *meta-analysis* (combining findings from several studies) of six cross-sectional and longitudinal studies. She compared the racial/ethnic identities of domestic TRAs with non-White, same-race adoptees and found that TRAs had significantly lower racial/ethnic identities than same-race adoptees. The lower racial/ethnic-identity finding, in turn, reflects other research showing TRAs to be highly acculturated to the White majority (Andujo 1988; Kim 1977). Interestingly, TRAs in some studies were classified as having strong and secure racial identities, yet they still reported at least some discomfort over racial appearance (Benson et al. 1994; Brooks and Barth 1999).

The studies on racial identity clearly suggest that opportunities to develop comfortable relationships with individuals from communities of origin are key in minimizing confusion over ethnic identity, and this confusion in turn is related to behavior problems and psychological distress for adoptees (Cederblad et al. 1999; Cross et al. 1991; Munford 1996; Yoon 2001). The following excerpt is typical of what many TRAs experience growing up in a White community. Notice the profound confusion over oneself. Tanya reports:

> Culture shock. That's what happens to me. My mom sent me out to St. Louis. I walked out of the airplane and there was nothing but African American people. I walked out there and I was sitting there going, "Oh my gosh, Oh my gosh." My sister took me around and I remember she took me to this place in St. Louis. My sister took me to this—I don't even know, it was in the inner city, it was scary. I was scared; I didn't even want to get out of the car. It's where drug addict mothers can drop their kids off and they take care of the babies. It's a place, a safe haven for kids, and I remember we kind of did some other work there, I helped feed the babies. We were there for probably about three hours. My sister, I remember she drove down to Wendy's saying, "I am so hungry we have to go to Wendy's." I was like, "I'm not getting out of the car; I'm scared. I don't want to get killed."

Later in the interview she expressed similar ideas: "I haven't experienced a black community. My friends—I want to move to [a larger, but still medium-size, city]; I've lived here all my life. I'm scared to move—I'm so used to this, I'm terrified of moving. That's probably my own psychological issues."

The degree to which adoptees have redressed cognitive racial dissonance is typically evaluated against and classified according to progressive stages of understanding and mastery of race, as outlined by various models of racial-identity development (Cross 1987; Cross et al. 1999; Erickson 1968; Phinney 1989). As Smith and colleagues (2008, 25) report, "Most models of African-American identity formation assume a strong black-focused identity is the most desired outcome." If "a strong black-focused identity is the most desired outcome," Tanya fails that test.

Another influential model of how Blacks acquire a racial identity is the model of nigrescence developed by William Cross (1980). Cross defines *nigrescence* as "the process of becoming black" (81). Cross's theory for African American racial-identity development posits that the simple act of being born in a Black body does not automatically ensure that the child will necessarily absorb, accept, and apply the received wisdom conveyed by Black parents through the racial-socialization process. Cross lays out five stages in his nigrescence model, with each stage reflecting a particular set of values, attitudes, and worldviews that characterize the process of racial-identity development for African Americans.

Preencounter is the first stage of Cross's nigrescense model. The world is viewed through a Eurocentric lens, which tends to degrade all things Black while idealizing Whiteness. The second stage is the *encounter* stage, wherein the individual experiences a life-changing event. This event serves as a catalyst that causes the individual to reinterpret his or her world and thus search for a Black identity. The third stage is *immersion-emersion*, a stage that has two distinct phases. In the *immersion* phase, the individual begins to immerse herself or himself in Black culture and terminate relationships with all things affiliated with Whites, to the extent possible. The individual begins to idealize all things affiliated with Blacks, while denigrating White people and White culture.

Emersion, in turn, is marked by the reeducation of the individual as she or he explicitly seeks to learn about Black culture and engages in building bridges of support with other like-minded Blacks. Individuals within this phase are generally less reactive and angry toward White people.

The fourth stage of Cross's model is *internalization*. Internalization enables Black people to develop a more secure and calm disposition. In this stage, Blackness continues to be the primary basis of group reference while the individual begins to approach the world more pluralistically and from a more inclusionary standpoint. In this stage, friendships with Whites begin to reemerge and are renegotiated.

The fifth and final stage is *internalization-commitment*, which tends to be characterized by Blacks engaging in political and activist types of activities to demonstrate a continued commitment to Black causes. Cross-cultural alliances with individuals and groups from different racial backgrounds often characterize this stage of Cross's model. The uplift of all, both in the group and out of the group, through the uplift of Black people is a common theme in this stage.

Thomas Parham and Janet Helms (1981) note, however, that people have a variety of attitudes characteristic of each stage, and thus an individual should not be classified in any one stage on the basis of his or her perhaps seemingly static beliefs or actions. Rather, they suggest, Cross's model, as well as other stage theories, should serve as a guide to better understanding Black identity as a series of statuses that do not necessarily occur linearly or individually. Individuals may, for example, simultaneously experience and reflect traits of more than one stage.

Stage theories, such as the model of nigrescence developed by Cross, can often be viewed as deterministic and often do not account for the dynamic and unique circumstances germane to Blacks from all over the country as individuals and as a group. Put simply, Blackness often looks very different depending on where one is positioned within geopolitical space and along the continuum of race, class, and gender.

The mixed results of racial-identity studies of transracial adoption illustrate the many contingencies and wide variability of factors that influence the development of a healthy sense of self as a Black person. As Kimberly DeBerry and colleagues (1996, 2376) suggest, "The essence of human development is the attainment of competence across hierarchically embedded ecological domains (e.g., home, school, society, and culture)."

For TRAs, then, a positive reference-group orientation to both U.S. society's White mainstream *and* the racial group of origin is imperative (DeBerry et al. 1996; Kallgren and Caudill 1993). "Reference group orientation, of which racial identity is one component, reflects decisions about which group(s) one prefers to be committed to in terms of values, attitudes, culture, and one's role in the group" (DeBerry et al. 1996, 2377).

The adoptees in our study vary greatly against this standard. As with biracial individuals who physically embody two historically conflicting worlds, TRAs live daily within one world while they physically embody the other world. As long as TRAs continue to live only in predominantly White communities, their self-conceptions and identity may never be challenged. Few, however, likely live in such arrangements. The formation of a racial identity equipped to effectively and simultaneously navigate the White world and the world of color is required for most. The formation of a bicultural identity can be difficult in a society such as the United States, one with historical stigmatization of ethnic minority groups (Friedlander et al. 2000; Pinderhughes 1995). The challenges of trying to simultaneously meet the expectations of two cultural groups are reflected in the degree to which a biracial or a transracially adopted individual develops a positive reference-group orientation for each of the two cultures (Cross 1985; Kerwin et al. 1993).

Pointedly, even children adopted at an older age tend to have strong identification with the White mainstream (Feigelman and Silverman 1984). At the same time, "identity confusion only occurs when the individual internalizes the conflict between the two cultures" (Friedlander et al. 2000, 188). At least six factors influence the level of healthy biracial-identity development, including (1) the degree of overlap between the two racial backgrounds; (2) the availability of cultural translators, models, and mediators; (3) the amount and type of feedback guiding the development of normative behavior for each racial group; (4) the match between the biracial individual and each group's conceptual and problem-solving approaches to the social; (5) the individual's degree of bilingualism; and (6) the degree of dissimilarity in phenotypic features (de Anda 1984). A cohesive biracial identity, however, is possible to develop (Kerwin et al. 1993). Indeed, Myrna Friedlander and colleagues (2000, 188) argue that young foster children who are exposed to two racial cultures naturally view themselves as biracial if their parents foster an open dialogue with them on the topic of race.

Only within recent years have social scientists expressed theories of biracial-identity development (Buckley and Carter 2004; Poston 1990; Root 1990). According to W. S. Carlos Poston (1990), a biracial individual typically moves from denying the salience of at least one of his or her two racial backgrounds, to actively struggling to choose one racial background over the other, to a gradual acceptance of both racial backgrounds. Maria Root (1990), in contrast, suggests that to develop a healthy biracial identity, an individual must be able to accept both racial backgrounds and declare how she or he self-identifies, and then develop strategies for coping with social resistance and questions about her or his choice of identity. Like Root, Robert Carter (1995) suggests that a biracial individual must begin with an acceptance of both racial backgrounds to develop a healthy biracial identity. Carter departs from Root, however, by suggesting that biracial-identity development is an ordered process that requires the development of positive acceptance of the less accepted racial background, and then the embracing of the more accepted racial background. Few empirical studies explore biracial-identity formation. As Peter Buckley and Martin Carter (2004, 47) note, biracial people face "unique emotional and psychological realities . . . that result from being raised by parents with different racial backgrounds in a society that treats race as a dichotomous variable." The same is true of those who are adopted transracially, or children of mixed heritage, for that matter.

Racial- and Cultural-Socialization Studies in Transracial Adoption

For TRAs, the development of a positive racial identity is profoundly influenced by the adopting parents' attitudes about and approaches toward addressing race and racism (McRoy and Zurcher 1983; DeBerry et al. 1996). As Smith and colleagues (2008, 27) note, "Recent [TRA] research has focused on parents' approaches to cultural and racial socialization, and has examined how different approaches affect aspects of their children's ethno-racial identity and psychological adjustment." These studies examine the connection between what adopting parents do to orient or socialize their adopted children to their cultural and racial groups of origin and the implications of these socializing practices on adoptees' identities and adjustment outcomes. Underlying these studies is the assumption that processes of cultural and racial socialization facilitate the development of cultural competence in adoptees. Some of the adoptive parents we interviewed were more successful at this socialization than others. Note the interview with one of the adoptees, Dinesha, now in her twenties:

> *Darron:* Did your parents do anything in particular that sort of prepared you for the kind of stares and looks and maybe comments that you may have received? Did they ever sit you down and say, "I'm going to give you a formal lesson on what to do when people stare at you"? Anything like that?
>
> *Dinesha:* No, and I think that's really the cool thing about it because they didn't make a big deal about it. Like, "You know what, you're just as good as everybody else." There wasn't ever, "Well you are different, you know, you are brown." No. Nothing like that, and I think that's why . . . I was so comfortable. Nobody treated me in the home differently, why should they treat me differently out there? So, no, not at all.

Dinesha seems to intimate that it was "cool" for her parents to not bring any undue attention to her color, and that they had a very strong colorblind approach, a laissez-faire position, on race. The message Dinesha got was, "Do nothing, don't bring attention to race, and there will be no problems." Further, Dinesha seemed to accept the lesson quite well. Notice at the end of the exchange she says, "Why should they treat me differently out there?"

In terms of identity issues and a healthy sense of who she is as a young woman, Dinesha clearly sees herself as socially White in every way. Notice an exchange a little later in the interview:

> *Darron:* Did you date much in high school?
>
> *Dinesha:* You know, I didn't. Since the past—my first date was a year and a half ago. I was never really interested in boys. I didn't really feel like boys were attracted to me.

Cardell: Why did you think boys weren't attracted to you?

Dinesha: I don't know. Maybe just because I wasn't the cookie-cutter kind of girl.

Cardell: You mean because you're brown? [She had called herself "brown" earlier.]

Dinesha: Because I'm Black, and just because I wasn't into the whole frilly pink. . . . And I know not all guys are into that, but it just wasn't what I saw most of the guys going for, whether it was color or not.

Cardell: So you started dating now. White guys?

Dinesha: Uh-huh.

Cardell: And no Black guys?

Dinesha: I'm not really attracted to Black guys. I mean, I don't know, just because I'm really White.

Cardell: That's what you're comfortable with, is dating White guys, because that's more—

Dinesha: What I've grown up around. And I'm sure if I grew up around more African Americans, I would be more attracted to them. You know, some are, and it's . . . I don't know.

Clearly, Dinesha's parents did very little to prepare her to confront, cope with, and resist racism. In fact, Dinesha acknowledges difference but sees this difference in minimal ways. Thus, minimization is one way that race plays out in the lives of adoptive parents and their children.

For African Americans reared in African American communities, however, cultural competence includes awareness, understanding, and implementation of coping strategies that are requisite for developing resilience against racism (DeBerry et al. 1996). White parents likewise must consider the challenges of racially socializing Black adoptees for cultural competence, awareness, and understanding, and the implementation of coping strategies. We address this topic in greater detail in the final chapter. As Lee (2003, 721) argues, "White parents, who often lack experience with minority communities, may not have first-hand knowledge and experience to teach their children about life as a racial or ethnic minority in society." Smith and colleagues (2008, 26) also note that "parents adopting transracial were more likely than not to minimize racial differences and emphasize a colorblind approach." Taking a race-neutral approach underemphasizes the experiences the adoptees are likely to have. Instead, transracial adopting parents typically assimilate the adoptees into the White mainstream culture, as was the case with Dinesha. The parents do not take an active role in helping adoptees integrate race as a positive source of strength, mainly because for White parents, race has not mattered in the same ways it does for Blacks (McRoy and Zurcher 1983; DeBerry et al. 1996; Lee 2003). As we have noted, families that adopt transracially tend to have higher educational and income levels than families with their own birth children. TRA children are likely reared in middle-class neighborhoods with relatively little contact with other children of the same race. Some of the parents were sensitive to this issue. Ms. White noted that too often her adopted son simply tried to emulate what he saw on television shows that provided few positive role models for young Black men. She commented: "Well, I wished that I would have moved [to a more diverse place] because, you see, my kids have thought that being Black meant you didn't go to school, you joined a gang, you were tough. Do you see what I'm saying?"

Notice also the conflict that occurred in an interview with Ms. Brown:

> *Cardell:* So then, in public schools? Would [your child] have gotten some exposure to Martin Luther King, and to other African American leaders?
>
> *Ms. Brown:* Not when she was at school. I think there's far more exposure now. I think in the last fifteen years it altered a great deal. So that where she got her education from was from us really. We made huge efforts to make sure she knew what was going on. But she's always found that side of the Black heritage very, very distressing.
>
> *Cardell:* That's interesting. Her school classes? Would she have been one of a few Blacks only; would she have been the only Black, or mixed ancestry person?
>
> *Ms. Brown:* It was . . . she wasn't the only Black child there. We lived in a White middle-class area. Generally the only mixed-ancestry person there. Except for the Asians. And then a Nigerian family moved in. Although none of the family was ever in her year. Children around, you know. We tried, we actually looked at several schools. We picked one that had the most Black faces in it. We aren't sure it was a wise choice. But it's been better for her to feel more at home.

Other research suggests that when children of color grow up in predominately White communities, they may experience racial prejudice and discrimination, which in turn may form the basis of higher rates of maladjustment and psychological problems (Hjern et al. 2002). Conversely, Dong Pil Yoon (2001) found that when adoptive parents took an active role in their adoptees' ethnicity, they were more likely to have a positive racial and ethnic identity. Race socialization, like all socializing processes, usually occurs through informal educational strategies. At times, it is explicit instruction, but mostly adoptees learn from the implicit ways their parents handle racial conflict themselves.

Lee (2003) provides a typology of four cultural-socialization strategies: assimilation, enculturation, child choice, and racial inculcation. While his focus is on Korean adoptees, they can easily be applied to African American adoptees. These are four different strategies the adopting parents can provide for their adoptees to help them make sense of race and ethnicity.

The strategy of cultural *assimilation* typically occurs with minimal parental effort because children are immediately and constantly exposed to majority culture. Lee (721) argues that a "variant of cultural assimilation is a humanistic strategy that emphasizes a 'colorblind' orientation or a view of humanity without reference to ethnicity or race." While this is a common strategy, it ignores the fact that the adoptee is likely to find that American society is not colorblind.

Lee identifies the second strategy as *enculturation*, a strategy that focuses on teaching adoptees about their birth cultures and heritage. More specifically, he argues that adoptive parents who focus on enculturation typically provide their children with a variety of educational, social, and cultural opportunities that are intended to instill "ethnic awareness, knowledge, pride, values, and behaviors, as well as to promote a positive ethnic identity" (2003, 722).

The third strategy identified by Lee is *child choice*. This strategy places the burden on the children to determine the extent to which they want to identify with a particular racial or ethnic group. This strategy has not been well researched and appears ineffectual. Given the heavy emphasis and responsibility placed on the child, this strategy fails to address the developmental appropriateness and decision making when the adoptees are young. As adults, their more mature decision-making skills likely help them choose their identity. This option is probably not available to African American children unless they are biracial and have more White than Black physical characteristics.

One of our interviewees, a young woman by the name of Susan, tried to adopt this strategy. Though she clearly had some African features, she was light skinned with freckles and wavy hair. In her school years she identified with, and hung out with, the White and Asian students. This despite the fact that she had several adopted brothers who were quite clearly African Americans.

The final socialization strategy is *racial inculcation*. According to Lee (2003), racial inculcation refers to the ways adopting parents attempt to teach TRAs to cope with and resist racism. Lee maintains, however, that "[t]here is limited empirical research on the extent to which transracial adoptive parents engage in racial inculcation" (2003, 722). The cultural-socialization opportunities that most adoptive parents provide for adoptees in early childhood tend to decline as adoptees grow into adolescence (Lee 2003; Mohanty et al. 2006).

Importantly, survival for African Americans and other Americans of color has historically required the ability of individuals and collectives to successfully understand and navigate both U.S. society's White mainstream and subjugated minority contexts, a condition referred to by W. E. B. DuBois (1917/2005) as *double-consciousness*. DeBerry and colleagues (1996, 2377), however, found that African American children were often socialized to be bicultural often as a matter of life and death. Similarly, White adoptive parents who have positive attitudes toward bicultural socialization of transracial adoptees are better prepared to foster bicultural competence in children of color (Friedlander et al. 2000; Phinney 1991; Thomas and Tessler 2007). This includes perceiving the family to be multiracial rather than White; facilitating the adoptees' access to multicultural events (e.g., trips to country of origin, visits to museums, attendance at cultural events); having social networks made up of individuals from the culture of origin (e.g., friends and acquaintances of the same racial background as the adoptee); and residing in a multiracial community with heterogeneous school populations. Smith and colleagues (2008, 27) also argue that racial adaptations of minority children with a bicultural or multicultural identification are the most highly adjusted.

We next provide a review of some of the literature on what Black parents do to racially socialize their children about their likely encounters with racism and microaggressions.

Racial Socialization and Black Parents

Descriptions of race socialization often emerge on the margins of research on the Black family's role in making children familiar with statuses, social roles, and prescribed behavior within society (Boykin and Toms 1985; Thomas and Speight 1999). Racial socialization occurs primarily among African Americans.

While other minority groups experience prejudice, discrimination, and other microaggressions, they experience less of these than do most African Americans. Thus, race socialization appears to be a distinctive, protective child-rearing practice for African Americans (Peters 1985; Thornton et al. 1990). It is the process whereby Black parents explicitly and implicitly transmit race-specific messages (e.g., values, norms, beliefs) and training to their children about living in a world where race and racial identity continue to shape life chances for Black Americans and other Americans of color (Brown and Lesane-Brown 2006; Demo and Hughes 1990; Greene 1992). Harriet McAdoo (2002) notes that parents often discuss racism and discrimination with their children so that the children can better deal with racial prejudice.

Diane Hughes and Lisa Chen (1999) describe several types of communications that minority parents have with their children. Some are verbal, some nonverbal. Some are deliberate communications, but many parents choose to engage their children in self-awareness, and some communications result from unintended incidents that lead the parents to discuss what happens in a racially conscious society. Others do not discuss racial issues with their children. Hughes and Chen categorize the various types of communication (see table 4.1). The results of the analysis show that African Americans are the most likely of the groups to talk to their children about racial issues. Such skills are important in dealing with racial situations that the child may encounter. Some parents model pride in their ethnic/racial tradition by encompassing traditionally ethnic behaviors in their life, by taking their children to cultural events, and by reading ethnic literature. (See also Marshall 1995.)

The results shown in table 4.1 are from a survey conducted in 1999 by Hughes and Chen (1999). While the survey included Black, Dominican, and Puerto Rican parents in New York and Chicago, the important results for our discussion are those regarding the African American parents. They show that almost all African American parents say they talk with their children about racism, encourage their children to be proud of their heritage, and engage in ethnic self-awareness activities with their children. Over 90 percent of the African American parents said they encouraged their children to be proud of their heritage and culture. Over 60 percent read books to their children about their history. Few, however, told their children that they should not trust Whites. And almost all encouraged their children to show respect to people of all backgrounds. For all except two of the questions (mistrust of Whites and telling the children they must be better than Whites), African American parents were significantly more likely than parents from the other groups to report that they did this prophylactic treatment for their children.

Table 4.1. Ways in Which Minority Parents Socialize Their Children about Race and Racism

	Puerto Rican Americans	*Dominican Americans*	*African Americans*	*Mexican Americans*
Cultural Socialization				
Have you ever encouraged your child to be proud of his/her own heritage and culture?	85.4	81.3	93.4	69.9
Do you ever do things with your child to remember events in [group's] history?	71.2	72.5	81.5	56.1
Have you ever read books to your child by [group's] authors or about [group's] history?	37.0	43.5	64.1	23.9
Preparation for bias				
Do you ever talk with your child about racism and discrimination against people in this country?	48.1	45.5	75.1	34.4
Do you ever tell your child that people will try to limit how far he/she can go in life because he/she is [group]?	14.0	25.2	53.3	8.8
Do you ever tell your child that some people might treat him/her badly or unfairly because he/she is [group]?	28.0	28.2	59.8	14.3
Do you ever tell your child that he/she has to be better than White children to get as far in life?	6.6	9.8	10.1	10.4
Promotion of mistrust				
Do you ever tell him/her that he/she should not trust White people?	5.1	4.9	4.4	5.6
Egalitarian values and perspective				
Have you ever encouraged your child to respect people from all different backgrounds?	90.1	85.3	94.6	84.2
Have you ever done or said things to show that all people are the same, regardless of race or ethnicity?	76.6	69.7	89.1	66.1

Source: Hughes and Chen (1999).

Since the White parents in our sample seldom experience racism themselves, fewer of them than the Black parents are likely to have these kinds of discussions with their children of color.

The specific ways that Black parents socialize their children are borne out of personal and group experiences over time (Boykin and Toms 1985; Ogbu 1985; Peters 1985). The interpersonal and intergroup experiences with Whites provide knowledge about how to cope with racism and thrive within hostile contexts. Racial socialization is more than race-specific messages and values; it is also about self-concept and ethnic and minority-group relations and roles within larger society.

Further, research suggests that racial socialization occurs at all income and educational levels. The amount of protection afforded children is related to the degree to which parents are able to help their children develop a well-grounded, positive racial identity (Peters 1985; Stevenson 1993). As noted in table 4.1, African American parents typically expect their children to consistently encounter both overt and backstage racism, despite their best efforts to insulate and protect them (Marshall 1995; Sanders-Thompson 1994). Accordingly, Black parents are cognizant of the need to prepare their children to outperform Whites for survival and any type of recognition within a White context—a condition of living referred to as *mundane extreme environmental stress*. In sum, the research suggests that when Black parents engage their children in racial socialization, there are positive psychological outcomes such as higher self-esteem, more positive racial and ethnic identities, and higher education achievement (Poindexter-Cameron and Robinson 1997; Spencer 1988; Thompson et al. 2000). Much of this teaching occurs as their children begin negotiating racial issues. The socialization invokes racial pride, and it occurs early and often in life (DeBerry et al. 1996; Thornton et al. 1990). As Hughes and Chen (1999) found, some parents focus on existing racial barriers (see also Bowman and Howard 1985; Branch and Newcombe 1986), and others on pride. Together the studies suggest that many Black parents instill a repertoire of strategies including adaptive reactions, coping styles, and adjustment tactics or techniques (Peters 1985; Thornton 1997).

So that their children can successfully survive racism and racial mistreatment, the parents provide them with love, a sense of safety, and the motivation to acquire a good education. Other factors typically deemed necessary to survive racism include the ability of parents to help their children develop a tough skin, high levels of tolerance, self-pride, and self-respect, without defaulting to victim roles and a belief that Whites will not reciprocate fair play.

The socialization, for African Americans, is achieved through a variety of mediums like parental attitudes, practices, and beliefs, and other social factors (Ogbu 1985). The specific content of the messages also varies depending on parents' age, gender, class, and income level (Fatimilehin 1999).

Wade Boykin and Forrest Toms (1985) classify Black families by the messages they transmit to their children. Those classified as *mainstream* generally socialize their children based on Eurocentric values and beliefs. Those in the second category, *minority*, are characterized by a degree of acceptance of oppressive and racist beliefs; these families are willing to work within a racist framework. Finally, the families in the third category of *race socialization* emphasize Black culture, even emphasizing West African traditions that embodied the importance of spirituality, harmony, movement, verve, affect, communalism, expressive individualism, oral traditions, and social perspective.

Academic work has not examined or portrayed the factors that prompt parents' discussions about race. And the question of whether the race-socialization process is a rite of passage or the result of a specific incident requires further research (Bowman and Howard 1985). In any case, the research literature bears out the supposition that the process of race socialization is a fundamental imperative to the development of a positive racial identity for African American children. An individual's relationship to a social group is always complex. The complexities of group identity and consciousness become further complicated when a child is adopted transracially and reared within the context of a racial group other than her or his own. In the remainder of this book we probe how well parents of TRAs are able to adequately socialize their adopted children about race and racism.

CHAPTER FIVE

Cross-Cultural Race Pioneers

White Adoptive Parents Learning and Not Learning about Race

I had never been around Black people in my whole life. I grew up in Vernal [Utah]. No Black people in Vernal.

—Mr. Collins, White adoptive father of Black daughter

I think some people don't even get that the Klan's negative. [They think] that's just history. My dad actually made a comment to me once that he was a card-carrying member of the Klan.

—Ms. Brown, White adoptive mother of Black children

Well, she [Ms. Stevens] grew up around people of color. She has two adopted Polynesian sisters that are fairly dark, but obviously Polynesian. She grew up on the Navajo reservation. So she's dealt all her life with different races.

—Mr. Stevens, White adoptive father of Black son

Don't be in a hurry to condemn because he doesn't do what you do or think as you think or as fast. There was a time when you didn't know what you know today.

—Malcolm X

LATER IN his life, Malcolm X pointed to the importance of thinking about someone's upbringing before condemning ignorance based on someone's lack of racial experience. As Malcolm would discover in his pilgrimage to Mecca, new experiences must be recognized before one can appreciate his or her own process of change as new knowledge is learned, gained, and applied. Many White adoptive parents do have an interest in their children's well-being and want to step outside their own environment; but there are limitations in place that thwart their efforts. We discuss these limitations in more detail in the pages to come. These parents, then, are left to rely on the social conditions and family backgrounds in which they grew up, and the notions about race and racial differences they inherited—conceptions of race as isolated, rigid, and inflexible, conceptions that are thus maladaptive to the realities of a diverse populace. Whether it is patently racist or openly accepting, the family home environment is a primary setting where each of us learns about racial issues. Accordingly, where we come from and the people we grow up with are central to what we know about race. We must seek out experiences that challenge our resolve, taking us out of our comfort zone in order to more effectively raise children of color, as well as to promote democracy of difference in our world.

Racial Knowledge: Going the Social Distance toward Race-Based Differences

Having racial knowledge is generally considered one of the primary qualifications required to effectively raise a Black child. Since White people in the United States tend to be geographically and socially isolated from people of color, the assumption is that White adoptive parents have little racial knowledge and are therefore disqualified from raising a Black child toward a positive identity. You can't teach what you don't know—as the old adage goes.

Hence, we wanted to know what kinds of backgrounds the adoptive parents had, and how these experiences influenced the ways they approached their roles as parents of Black children. We asked ourselves the following questions: Did the adoptive parents who grew up in racially isolated White neighborhoods feel they were or had been at a disadvantage in raising a Black child, as compared to the adoptive parents who grew up around and had experiences with people of color? Did the adoptive parents who had experiences with people of color draw on these cross-cultural experiences to help guide them in parenting? If so, how did they draw on these cross-cultural experiences, and what did the adoptive parents who had few or no experiences with people of color do to overcome this lack of cross-cultural experiences?

Table 3.1. The Adoptive Parents' Cross-Cultural Experiences and Backgrounds

Family Self-Reporting	*Background and Cross-Cultural Experiences of Parent(s)*	*Required Formal Training and Preparation for Transracial Adoption*	*Formal Involvement with Racial Diversity since Transracial Adoption*	*Informal Involvement with Racial Diversity since Transracial Adoption*
T1 Collins family	None	Classes as part of screening process for adoption	None	None
T2 March family	Both: none	Both: screening process for adoption only	Wife: presenter, trainer who teaches classes at the state level preparing future transracial adoptive parents for adoption process	Wife: self-selected, voluntary participation in classes, conferences; avid reader of books; has developed friendships with people of color; works in the school as a volunteer parent assistant
T3 Brown family	Wife: comes from a family she reports as racist; grew up in Utah Husband: comes from a family he reports as not racist; grew up in the Deep South during Jim Crow era	Both: screening process for adoption only	Wife: works on adoption cases as professional and leader of local advocacy groups Husband: adoption attorney	Wife: cohosts radio show focused on diversity issues; avid reader; attends conferences; develops friendships with people of color; works in the school as a volunteer parent assistant
T4 White family	None; grew up in Utah Former husband: none; grew up in Utah	None Former husband: none	Works professionally as a social worker on transracial adoptions Former husband: adoption attorney	Founder of advocacy group for African Americans and for raising Whites' awareness about African Americans; parent volunteer in schools; started African American fairs and culture camps in her community; started statewide endeavor to recruit African American parents to adopt Black children

(continued)

Table 5.1. *(continued)*

Family Self-Reporting	*Background and Cross-Cultural Experiences of Parent(s)*	*Required Formal Training and Preparation for Transracial Adoption*	*Formal Involvement with Racial Diversity since Transracial Adoption*	*Informal Involvement with Racial Diversity since Transracial Adoption*
T5 Hansen family	Both: none; grew up in Utah	Both: none	Both: none	Wife: president of local advocacy group for African Americans and transracial adoption; works in schools as a volunteer parent assistant
T6 Stevens family	Wife: grew up on an American Indian reservation Husband: none; spent time in air force as a young adult	Both: none	Both: none	Both: work in schools as volunteer parent assistants
T7 Ross family	Both: none; grew up in Utah	Both: none	Wife: works professionally as a social worker	Wife: works in schools as a volunteer parent assistant
T8 West family	Both: none; grew up in Utah Husband: spent time in military as a young adult	Both: none	Both: serve as presenters and trainers for transracial adoption at state level; serve as child advocates for Utah	Wife: works in schools as a volunteer parent assistant
T9 Davis family	Grew up in England	None	Is a well-known national speaker and advocate and authority on transracial adoption	Does community service in schools
T10 Vest family	Both: none; grew up in Utah	Both: none	Husband: is a presenter and trainer for families adopting transracially; is a published author on the topic of race and adoption	Both: avid readers; live in a culturally diverse neighborhood; have developed friendships with African Americans

As represented in table 5.1, the adoptive parents who participated in our study came from a range of different backgrounds and had a range of different experiences and knowledge about race and racism. Table 5.1 provides a general overview of the adoptive parents' respective cross-cultural experiences. The adoptive parents' cross-cultural experiences and knowledge are significant because they hint at and lay the foundation for the task of being White and taking responsibility for raising a happy, healthy, well-adjusted Black child who is prepared to address the realities of racial hostilities.

As suggested by the demographics on the adoptive parents' backgrounds, there is a wide range in the amount and types of cross-cultural experiences and exposure that the adoptive parents brought to the task of raising Black children. Mr. Collins, on one end of the continuum, came from a background that he felt provided him with no opportunities at all for contact with people of color, including African Americans. Having no cross-cultural experiences, as he explains in the epigraph at the opening of this chapter, Mr. Collins felt that he had very little knowledge about racial matters to bring to the task of raising his Black daughter. Similarly, Ms. Brown indicated that she grew up within a context largely devoid of contact with people of color and opportunities for cross-cultural friendships. Having a family member explicitly associated with the prejudice against people of color put forth by the Ku Klux Klan, however, Ms. Brown suggests that she was further hindered from developing knowledge about race. Referring to his wife, Mr. Brown explained, "She grew up around some Hispanic people, but no Black people. So she really did come the farthest."

Mr. Brown's assessment of his wife's background and limited opportunities for cross-cultural experiences points to the learning process as a distance that has to be traveled by individuals to arrive at racial knowledge. Ms. Brown had to travel a great distance; Mr. Brown, by contrast, felt that he himself had not traveled as far toward racial knowledge, due to his own background.

At the opposite end of the continuum, Mr. Brown described his background as rich with opportunities to develop racial knowledge. Referring to his upbringing and childhood, Mr. Brown stated, "I grew up in the South, and my father was probably the least prejudiced man that I've ever met. I could tell you stories." Growing up in the American South and having a father who was not prejudiced, Mr. Brown suggests that he started his journey toward racial knowledge much closer to the finish line than his wife did, because his surroundings offered him many opportunities for contact with people of color, particularly African Americans, and he did not have the barriers of race hate in his family to overcome as did his wife. Mr. Stevens likewise posits that his wife's background, growing up with adopted Polynesian sisters, has afforded Ms. Stevens greater racial knowledge than other Whites because she has had many more opportunities for cross-cultural interactions due to her extensive contact with people of color, albeit not specifically with African Americans.

A Continuum of Experiences with Race and Racial Differences

The adoptive parents thus saw themselves as coming to the task of raising a Black child with differing amounts of racial knowledge. The amount of racial knowledge a person has, it was presumed among the adoptive parents, is contingent upon the degree to which that person has had opportunities to interact with persons of color. The greater the contact with diverse persons, the greater the racial knowledge acquired, and the shorter the distance to travel in terms of being prepared to raise a Black child.

Some of the parents had had a wealth of opportunities to interact with people of color because they grew up in places like the American South or Native American Indian reservations, where larger numbers of people of color reside. Other parents, by contrast, grew up in racially isolated White communities. For some of the adoptive parents, adulthood mirrored a childhood of racial isolation within almost exclusively White settings. Many of the parents in this study had little or no significant contact with African Americans or other Americans of color even at the "occasional acquaintance" level. Yet research on White friendships with African Americans suggests that Whites often inflate their acquaintance-level relationships with Blacks, presenting them as more than the casual interactions that they are (Jackman 1986).

The racial isolation of predominately White settings among the adoptive parents is underscored by the fact that for many individuals, first contact with African Americans did not occur until the adoption of their Black child. The experiences of Mr. and Ms. West, as they explain below, suggest that their newly adopted Black child represented the first contact with people of color not only for themselves, but also for their neighbors and other members of the community where they lived:

> *Mr. West:* You know, when we were going to adopt [our daughter], our social worker brought a Black social worker with her, and we had quite an interesting conversation. She asked us all these same questions—how we were going to do this and that. And she said, "I have to tell you, in Farmington, Utah, there were no Black people."

> *Mr. West:* Our kids were the first [Black people] that ever spent the night in this town.
>
> *Ms. West:* Yeah, I'm proud of that. And now, there's lots more [Black people]. Well, not lots more [laughing], but there are more.

The novelty among White people of seeing and coming into contact with a Black person for the first time is evident in the story recounted by Mr. and Ms. West; it is also reminiscent of the experience James Baldwin (1985) describes in "Stranger in the Village," about his being a "sight" for the villagers of a tiny Swiss hamlet where apparently no Black man had ever previously set foot. Baldwin's commentary on his experience and reaction may be instructive on the topics of what it is like to be the racial other, and the spectacle of White fascination with racial differences. "In all of this, in which it must be conceded there was the charm of genuine wonder and in which there was certainly no element of intentional unkindness, there was yet no suggestion that I was human: I was simply a living wonder" (Baldwin, 1985, 81).

Pointedly, this newness of contact with people of color was not always or immediately seen as a limitation or potential disadvantage by the adoptive parents who came into transracial adoption with cross-cultural experiences. Indeed, many of the adoptive parents with few cross-cultural experiences posited that they had not realized they were expected or *supposed* to have had any experiences with people of color beforehand. Describing her first years as a White adoptive parent of a Black child, Ms. White recalled:

> We got our first Black children in '79, and we heard about NACAC [North American Council of Adoptable Children]; we didn't even know what it was. We had absolutely no preparation from LDS [Latter-day Saint] Family Services. I mean, we could have been adopting a purple child with green hair; they didn't have a clue, but at least we were somewhat astute. We realized we needed help, so we went to NACAC in Houston, Texas, and I remember sitting in the class—[a] Black social worker was teaching it on transracial parenting. And when she found out that our children were just a year old, she suggested we give them back. She said don't even try it, because you'll never do it. There's no way two little bumpkins from Utah could properly prepare Black children to live in this world, and I just remember sitting there, being so stunned . . . that she thought we couldn't do it, and that there were actually people that believed that. So, that was a great eye-opener for me, and that's when we started a group for African American awareness back in 1980 to help learn and to get other people that had adopted.

The experiences of Mr. and Ms. White are significant because it was their newly acquired awareness of their limited experience with racial differences and experiences that led them to seek out opportunities to learn about African Americans, their culture and history, and how to better parent a Black child. The impetus for learning about Black culture, therefore, did not come from any institutions or programs charged with helping Mr. and Ms. White learn the particulars of transracial adoption. The Whites' experiences came from seeking out members of the Black community kind enough to impart wisdom on the subject of raising a Black child.

Ms. White's reaction of being "stunned" at the African American social worker's negative evaluation of their ability to raise a Black child is also highly instructive. Knowledge of the consequences of race and racism was so far removed from Ms. White's daily experiences and thinking that she had not previously considered that she could possibly be unqualified to raise a Black child—hence her deep surprise at having her parenting abilities as a White adoptive parent questioned. Her eyes were opened because the response of the Black social worker caused her to begin thinking about issues of race and racism for the first time; her awareness of race and racism was raised. Had Ms. White had regular sustained contact with other people of color prior to this incident with the Black social worker, she might not have been quite so surprised: she might have known that usually Black people and people of color in general are already quite aware of and rarely surprised about the need to address matters of race and racism with prospective White people willing to engage the question of difference.

As the experiences of Ms. White suggest, having no experiences with people of color was not necessarily a condition that remained permanent among the adoptive parents. To paraphrase Malcolm X, there was a time when they, the adoptive parents, didn't know what they know today. Ms. White, like many of the adoptive parents in our study, not only began to search out opportunities to learn about race, but also went on to help many other White adoptive parents learn about the importance of race beyond the adoption process.

Mr. Vest is a published author who works with a colleague going around the country presenting workshops for predominantly White audiences on racial issues. Ms. March now has extensive experience organizing, attending, and presenting at seminars and conferences on transracial adoption. Ms. Brown, likewise, presents at events on her knowledge about transracial adoption, and has gone on to run radio broadcasts and book clubs on diversity issues related to African Americans and White parents raising Black children. Many of the adoptive parents who participated in this study continue to be active members, some serving as officers and leaders, in local and statewide organizations designed to support and educate transracially adoptive families.

The idea of White people teaching other White people about race and racism is an interesting one that is not necessarily as straightforward as it may initially appear. Historically, the burden has been on Blacks to convince White people, the dominant group, that indeed racism still exists and has horrendously painful and terrible consequences in the lives of its targets. On the one hand, it appears to be a sign of great progress that White people are teaching other Whites about racial issues, thus taking the burden off people of color. Since people of color did not create racism and since racism is not a threat for White people, it is extremely helpful to see White people teaching other Whites about race, racism, and racial mistreatment.

On the other hand, the potential of transracial adoption to serve as a venue for the continued privileging of Whiteness is also apparent with White people teaching other Whites about race and racism. In our society, images, beliefs, assumptions, and references depicting Black families as pathological and dysfunctional are everywhere circulating in the media and throughout daily conversations and interactions. That Black children are taken out of homes at rates far higher than White children reflects the power of negative representations of Black families to influence the actions of individuals. Since Black people are not typically seen as good parents in our society, White people have often presumed that they know better than Black people regarding what is best for Black children.

Accordingly, transracial adoption becomes yet another space where White people know not only what is best for Black children but also more than Black people about raising Black children; transracial adoption becomes a space by, for, and about White people—White people who happen to be parenting Black children. Black people themselves become an unnecessary part of the transracial-adoption equation, except in their role of providing the Black children who need homes. They are not in the role of people with expertise about what it means to raise a Black child, and about daily life with the indignities of racism.

Knowledge about Race Is Proximity to People of Color

Growing up in racially isolated White areas, according to the adoptive parents' self-reports, did not always mean that individuals never had opportunities to develop racial knowledge or have cross-cultural experiences. However, for most adoptive parents, the majority of cross-cultural experiences did not come until they became adults and moved out of their childhood homes and away from the communities they grew up in. Mr. Stevens's experience as an airman in the United States Air Force provided him with the opportunity to be the one White member of an otherwise all–African American basketball team. He explained:

> Having been raised mostly in Utah, I never had a chance to really interface with African Americans at all, till I got in the service. And then I played on a basketball team where I was the only White. I played . . . on the air-force basketball team on the military base. We'd play like North Dakota and stuff like that. And I was the only White guy on the team. I had literally, really, no experience with African Americans other than that basketball team.

Playing basketball and becoming part of a team facilitated cross-cultural experiences for Mr. Stevens. Traveling around the country and playing basketball provided Mr. Stevens with the opportunity for the first time in his life to regularly interact and work in close proximity with African Americans.

Like Mr. Stevens, Mr. West had also spent time in the air force. The military experiences likewise provided Mr. West with his first cross-cultural relationships with African Americans. He recalled,

> I've slept on the floor of Black people's homes. I've chopped cotton with Black people. I've picked cotton with Black people, and I have way better than the average [White person's knowledge of Black culture]. When I was in the military, my bunkmate was Black because I would accept a Black bunkmate when other people wouldn't. And this makes a big difference because I understand the culture. In the 1950s when I was in the air force, I had to cross the South with my bunkmate who was Black. Do you know what it's like to go through Arkansas and Tennessee in the 1950s, early '50s? I mean, this was . . . if I had not been able to function in the Black community. . . . It was because the military was totally integrated.

Neither Mr. Stevens nor Mr. West grew up around people of color, yet the military was a watershed moment in understanding difference. The environment and demands of military life create conditions whereby Whites and African Americans can work side by side, having ample opportunity to interact with the potential to develop lasting friendships of equal status.

Mr. Stevens's comfort level is inferred through the association of basketball and playing together with Black teammates as an equal member of the team. To play together on a team and in a game often presupposes comfort among members due to the cooperative teamwork required to win a game of basketball. Mr. West specifically identifies how he gained his familiarity and comfort with African Americans through hard and equal work of chopping cotton; traveling in the South, a region known for its vitriolic racism against Blacks; and the daily routines of sleeping on the floors of homes belonging to African Americans. Pointedly, Mr. West also goes on to establish a difference between himself and other Whites by noting how, unlike other Whites of the times, he would accept a Black bunkmate. The emphasis on daily routines and equality between himself and African Americans is proof that Mr. West has "racial knowledge" now, even if he did not have any as a child growing up in a racially isolated White community.

Contact with African Americans was put forth by the adoptive parents, as illustrated by Mr. West, as evidence that White people did not have personal and racial prejudices toward people of color, and most specifically not against African Americans. Hence, close proximity to and contact with people of color defines the possession of racial knowledge and the absence of racial prejudice. Thus, when the social distance between Whites and people of color becomes closed, White people have arrived at their full moral potential by having overcome their negative racial views. So within this perspective of full racial knowledge as directly tied to proximity of racial differences, we are all now getting along. Yet, while it always seems preferable to have feelings of mutual warmth and respect between Whites and people of color, there are some limitations regarding this idea of friendship between the races as an achieved solution to matters of race and racism.

During the era of chattel slavery when Whites enslaved African Americans, there were frequently mutual feelings of warmth and interpersonal regard between individual Whites and individual Blacks. It was not uncommon over many generations to have a Black woman working in the capacity of nanny and house servant, caring for a White woman's child. Ironically, however, these feelings of mutual regard and affection did not usually result in the manumission of slaves. Planters, a particular class of slave owners, often had children by their Black female slaves and cared very much for their offspring, sending them to Europe to acquire an education. Yet all of these warm emotions and acts of support and assistance did not change the realities of unequal power between Whites and Blacks as a group.

Since slavery times, Black women have generally continued low-level domestic-type jobs that are minimum wage and apply their labor to further the interests of Whites—housekeeping, janitorial work, and so on. The institutional structures of society create a vicious cycle of poor-quality education, housing, and health care that disproportionately affect people of color, thus locking Blacks and other racial minorities into these low-status jobs and positions within society. Therefore, warm feelings between individuals, while certainly preferable to bad feelings, have not changed and do not change the power dynamics of which group members have the wherewithal to access society's valued resources, goods, and opportunities to influence what is defined as good, true, and beautiful. Just as the Romans allowed those they subjugated to carry on with their cultural practices largely without interference, until the line was crossed confronting authority and domination and the hammer of military force came down swiftly, so too in our society have individuals managed to get along with each other nicely without disturbing the actual unequal power dynamics of who controls society.

Another limitation is that there is more trouble with friendship between the races when we consider carefully the idea that Whites have learned to "tolerate" and "get along with" people of color. The adoptive parents in this study, unlike most Whites, realize that among themselves there is a long and persistent history of racial animus against Blacks perpetuated by Whites. When Whites learn to overcome their reticence to be around Blacks and other racial minorities, they are seen as good and progressive. Whiteness, therefore, remains at the center of transracial adoption because the assumption that there was something bad about Blacks and people of color in the first place is never challenged. The centering of Whites in this friendship paradox is underscored if we reverse the idea and consider what it might be like if it were Blacks that had to learn to "tolerate" Whites, and we celebrated the idea that Whites were finally becoming "just like us Blacks."

Most Whites feel indignant at the idea that people of color must learn to accept them and at any hint of the idea that people of color do not like White people just because they are White; yet they think nothing of it when they act and talk in ways that manifest assumptions of Black inferiority, assuming that a Black man is going to rob or rape you if you are a White woman, that a Black woman is bossy and mean, that a Black man and a Black woman together in public couldn't possibly be married to each other so she must be his baby momma, and so on. As we have noted, White people can and often do have their individual Black friends whom they care deeply for as people, while continuing to hang on to assumptions that *this* Black person, *this* Black friend, is different from other Black people.

An individual's ability to get along with others is certainly important. Yet the ability to get along with people different from ourselves is a limited idea when considering that we still live in a society and world that are exceedingly divided by color. No matter where we go on this globe, darker skin color is always correlated with poverty and human suffering. For friendship to be something more than interpersonal feelings of warmth and regard we have to take a look at the institutional practices and the ways society is organized to keep the existing racial hierarchy in place. The adoptive parents in this study did want to do more than learn to have warm feelings for people of color and African Americans in particular. Nonetheless, there were very few formal opportunities for them to further their learning about racial differences and the differences that differences make.

Adoptive Parents Seeking Out Cross-Cultural Learning Experiences

As with their formative years and daily life as adults with generally few cross-cultural experiences, the legal process of adopting transracially also provided limited opportunities for the parents to expand their racial knowledge and experiences. Although all of the parents reported having undergone at least some degree of formal screening for adopting their children, none reported any prerequisite training or preparatory courses to complete the legal process of adoption. "We had absolutely no preparation from [the agency]," recalled Ms. White.

Ms. Brown and her husband likewise felt they had no preparation for transracial adoption and, thus, had to seek learning on their own. "I didn't know I didn't know anything," said Ms. Brown. Mr. Brown concurred: "She didn't know anything from [caring for African American] hair to whatever. So she immersed herself on skin [care], the whole business. Because she said, 'I don't know. I've got to know.'"

Mr. Collins was the only adoptive parent who reported receiving any type of preparation for raising children of color as part of the adoption process. He recalled the following:

> When we went through the classes, you know, for biracial adoption, they told us that maybe you'd have to move out of neighborhoods. They said you want to make sure you check with your family and make sure it's okay with the family, because they said one hundred years from now, when somebody's doing genealogy, if they find one Black person, the whole family's Black.

The training Mr. Collins received was a general strategy for testing the long-term racial biases of the family, rather than day-to-day strategies for raising Black children. Mr. Collins learned, from attending classes on transracial adoption and following through on advice to check with his family about their feelings on bringing a Black child into the family, that some White people (e.g., his relatives) might have some reservations about his efforts to adopt a child of color. According to Mr. Collins, the day-to-day realities of raising a Black child were not addressed in the transracial-adoption classes he attended.

Although the adoptive parents were not encouraged or given any training or preparation for raising Black children, they often used strategies to address what they believed was their limited level of cross-cultural experiences and knowledge. In many cases, the adoptive parents, the mothers in particular, simply went up to individual African Americans in public spaces, introduced themselves, and directly asked for knowledge about and assistance with raising Black children. For example, Ms. Hansen recalled, "At first, we would go out for dinner, and I would go up to a lady in the restaurant and say, 'This is my foster baby. I want to do the best for this child. Can you tell me what to use, what to do, how to do her hairstyles?'"

Ms. Brown remembered varying this strategy by seeking out an African American woman who worked in a public-service position in the state government, and calling at her office. Ms. Brown said,

> The first thing I did was I called [an African American woman], and she spent three hours on the phone. She was not easy on me. She said, "These children don't have a chance. Do you have any idea how devastating. . . ." She was intense, and I just listened and I took notes and I wrote. And then I went to a class that was being taught [on] how to raise antiracist children or something.

Ms. March went even further to introduce herself to African American women and then attempted to maintain and foster friendships with them.

She explained, "I felt I needed, as a mother of Black children—I needed Black women to help me normalize what it means to be Black for my children."

Many of the adoptive parents, again the mothers in particular, also read books, went to conferences, and became members of advocacy groups for transracial adoption as other strategies for addressing what they felt was their limited number of experiences. In many cases, the adoptive mothers became the presidents and leaders of the advocacy groups they joined. Ms. Brown explained the following:

> I went to [the advocacy group] for the first time. They had no one in the [youth division]. But there were all these children, and I had children. And I said, "Well, let me plan some activities." Before you knew it, I was president for eight years. They became my dearest friends, and I was in a minority setting with Black leadership trying to create resources for these families and kids. And I'm a very avid reader, so I read lots of books by Black authors. Then I would find them and interview them on a local radio show.

Mr. and Ms. West likewise worked at the state level as representatives of Utah advocating for adopted children. Mr. West explained, "We were the child advocates for Utah for some years." Ms. Hansen also recalled, "I was the president at [group name] for about ten years. And the majority of the families who adopt Black children who are [religious identity] go there for a type of resource. I was also president of an organization that advocates for transracial-adoptee families of African Americans."

Four of the adoptive parents, Mr. Vest, Ms. March, Ms. White, and Ms. Davis, also taught cultural-diversity lessons for adoptive parents under the auspices of state-sanctioned agencies. "When we teach these transracial classes, we tell people, 'You have to think about where you live,'" Mr. Vest explained. Thinking about where you live presumes that you are thinking about race since White people tend to live in racially isolated areas. Mr. Vest's expectation that White adoptive parents of children of color will think about where they live is important in that they are learning about issues of race and racism, which are significant components of raising Black children, and how to address them.

The 1994 passage of the Multiethnic Placement Act (Public Law 103-382) prohibits "the delay or denial of a child's foster care or adoptive placement *solely* on the basis of race, color, or national origin" (Smith et al. 2008, 15; emphasis in the original). Not wanting to be identified as operating outside of the law, adoption agencies continue to have vested interests in not requiring prospective adoptive parents to undergo any type of training for adopting a child culturally and racially different from themselves. Doing so would treat Black children and other children of color differently, in violation of the law. Many adoption agencies have therefore stayed away from imposing courses, seminars, and lessons to prospective adoptive parents altogether. This is a clear case of the law working against the interests of the children in favor of privileging the White parents. There have been efforts at repealing and amending the aforementioned law for the purposes of better preparing parents for dealing with a myriad of racial issues that remain perniciously real.

The adoptive parents' limited formal training for transracial adoption is hardly surprising, due to the consequences of the law. The adoptive parents, as we have noted, come from backgrounds with varying degrees of cross-cultural experiences and contact with people of color, African Americans in particular. It is significant, then, that regardless of their background, the majority of the adoptive parents nevertheless still wanted and used various strategies to seek out further opportunities to learn more about race and racism and African American culture and practices.

The adoptive parents were largely in agreement on the significance of the need for addressing matters of race and racism, regardless of differences in their backgrounds in terms of greater or fewer opportunities for contact with and proximity to people of color growing up. They wanted and sought out more knowledge and learning opportunities, even without the encouragement of or support from institutions such as adoption agencies, and even in the presence of constraining laws governing transracial adoption. Because formal opportunities to learn about race and racism have been limited, the adoptive parents developed and used strategies on their own to acquire that knowledge.

The willingness of these adoptive parents to not only learn about race and racism, but to seek out further learning opportunities, is telling. The adoptive parents had a vested interest in doing so because they wanted to do everything possible to be effective parents for their Black children. Whereas White people in general tend to be stubbornly resistant to learning about race and racism, these White adoptive parents wanted and sought out more opportunities. The adoptive parents wanted to close the gap between themselves and racial knowledge. They were aware of the fact that to teach about race you need to know about race.

Summary

Without question, the adoptive parents who participated in our study are highly competent, caring, conscientious, concerned, and warm individuals who love their children, both adopted and biological. These parents work hard to successfully provide for their children and want them to grow up to be happy, healthy, and responsible adults. Yet there are challenges to overcome when raising Black children. White adoptive parents must unlearn and develop a critique of Whiteness. Even a cursory awareness of race and privilege gave the parents an advantage over the general White population, who essentially have no vested interests beyond that of the casual outside observer or tourist. The highly segregated communities where the adoptive parents were typically raised, and tend to still live even after the adoption of their Black children, often make meaningful experiences and regular contact with African Americans difficult to achieve. As parents of African American children, they have generally continued to live in highly racially isolated White communities, with only superficial and occasional contact with individuals of African descent. Some of the adoptive parents have developed and maintained friendships with African Americans while working together in community, religious, and other public settings.

In general, the adoptive parents recognized, and worked hard to address and overcome, what they identified as the problem of their limited cross-cultural background experiences and knowledge. Many of the adoptive parents, the mothers in particular, have become leaders in their communities, advocating for their own adopted children as well as for transracially adopted children in general. In subsequent chapters, we take a look at some of the ways the background demographics and cross-cultural experiences of the adoptive parents may have influenced their efforts to raise their Black children.

CHAPTER SIX

White Parents Teaching Black Children about Race

My parents used to take us—my mom rented *Roots*. She made sure we knew Martin Luther King, *Amistad*, whatever, everything . . . and black camps. My parents used to take my siblings up there and they'd stay up there for weekends.

—Nykia, Black female adoptee

About the hair thing, I just told them [TRAs]: you are different in that respect. Your hair is different than theirs and you just need to know that they've never experienced this before. But they still have no right to be touching you. It's your body, and they're curious, and you can explain things to them.

—Ms. Hansen, White adoptive mother

Well, and there's folks that come and they just want to look through the glass and they don't really want a lot; they just want to look at you and see how different you are. And there are the ones who really are genuine, and I teach my kids about that: What do you think the motivation is here? Did this person mean to hurt you? Were they just uneducated and they didn't know better? So we can choose to educate them, to ignore them, but we won't engage with—if a person's just being mean to be flat-out mean, that's their problem.

—Ms. March, White adoptive mother

THE PARENTS we interviewed reported strong desires and efforts to teach their African American adopted children about race. Thus, the ways in which the White parents actually teach their children about our nation's racial history and the racial mistreatment largely directed at Black Americans were examined. What are the race lessons they teach to their adopted children?

Race Lessons

One way White parents teach race lessons to their adoptive children is by presenting a collection of distinctive strategies about their birth culture, thus preparing them to cope with the realities of racism and the burdens of living in a Black body. In general, we identified three interrelated themes, each carrying a specific meaning or lesson about race made concrete through daily practices: (1) celebrating diversity, (2) caretaking Whites, and (3) getting along with Whites. The three race lessons are not mutually exclusive, but rather fluid and dynamic.

Celebrating Diversity: Be Proud of Who You Are and Where You Come From

Among the adoptive parents we interviewed there was near consensus that TRAs and their family members should take pride in the cultural and racial backgrounds of adoptees. As one father indicated, "Well, see now, we wanted them to be proud of who they were and where they came from." Having cultural pride was so important for some adoptive parents that it was described as a human right. As Ms. March stated, "They deserve to be able to be proud of who they are and [to] be able to relish, in the history that they have and the culture that they have, the strong individuals that have come from that, and sometimes I feel sad about the fact that there's some that won't know that."

Research on transracial adoption has demonstrated that adoptive parents want their sons and daughters to affirm their race and cultural pride (Lee 2003; Thompson et al. 2000; Thornton 1997). Cultural pride for these parents is framed as an individual thing, a constituent of their being, something the adoptee should inherently possess. Cultural pride is not what Black adoptees receive as members of the larger African American community. It is not about the "love of, and the loyalty to our Race" (Floyd 1925, as cited in Harris 1992, 277). The TRA families live in isolation from the larger African American community and are not part of a community of color. The only time many of the adoptees had an opportunity to meet, mix with, and mingle with other African Americans was when their parents took them to "cultural camps" that were held for a day or at most a few days. Even then, the other African American children there were mostly other TRAs.

In many ways, the TRA experience is similar to that described by Beverly Tatum (2004) when African American children reared in the suburbs later attended the University of California, Berkeley. They did not know how to relate to other African American students. In other words, the adoptees lacked the ability to "code switch," that is, recognize the prose, norms, values, and experiences encountered when living in a vibrant Black community of friends, relatives, strangers, and acquaintances. The adoptive parents taught their children from a White Western perspective of *individualism*, the pursuit of individual rather than collective goals. This perspective limited their abilities to make connections between unequal systemic conditions, negative stereotypes, and cultural representations of African Americans that have historically legitimized racial mistreatment, the factors that have made cultural pride and racial-group uplift necessary in the first place.

As a group, the adoptive parents expected TRAs to draw on cultural pride as a source of personal strength and a tool for combating racial mistreatment. Adoptees were to develop cultural pride by aspiring toward an inventory of exemplary African Americans; they could not just be themselves. At the beginning of this chapter we related an example of one parent teaching her son about racial pride. Mr. Stevens gave us another example during an interview. He explained,

> [My son] has this, uh, book of famous Black people who've accomplished things. There's a lot of Black women too that have done some wonderful things. I said to [my son], "Realize that these people did things. Like George Washington Carver. Think what he did against all that adversity." We just got through reading, uh, Robinson . . . baseball player . . . Frank Robinson? [Darron: No, it's Jackie.] Jackie. We just read it, but I said, "Think what he went through and how he handled it." I said, "This is a man." I said, "Think how he handled it. This is a man you can look up to. In spite of all the things they made him do as a professional baseball player. Probably the best baseball player in his time! I mean, he broke every record."

In other words, the lives and stories of individual African Americans were interpreted and spoken as stories of merit. These heroes clearly were superb individuals. The lesson, when framed as "pulling themselves up by the bootstraps," is that individualism is important; George Washington Carver and Jackie Robinson became, as Elizabeth Spelman (1988) notes, *just like us* (Whites). By using the principle of merit to understand race, the White adoptive parents did not teach about the structural and historical relations within society that enable the hard work of African Americans and other people of color to remain in the margins, or, more importantly, about the fact that White work means something very different from Black work.

In order to teach TRAs about their birth culture and foster cultural pride, the parents utilized culture camps, fairs, and trips, and exposed their children to African American role models through books and sometimes films. Ms. Ross noted, "We had cultural nights where the whole family would go out and we'd do a Black-culture evening." Similarly, Ms. White mentioned some of the funeral homes operated by African Americans: "It was neat to drive down there to show my kids that culture. I wanted them to see it. You know, look at the way they do things; they are eccentric and I think it's great." By exposing their adoptees to African American culture, the parents expected the adoptees to pick up an understanding of that culture through osmosis.

The adoptive parents understood culture as a resource that they did not have, because they were not Black, but that they wanted to provide for their adopted children. The individualism of the adoptive parents guided them toward passive cultural-socialization practices. The adoptive parents and TRAs became cultural tourists, doing "drive-bys of Blackness" with windows rolled up. In many ways, the adoptive parents seemed to want to provide TRAs with Blackness minus the historical and contemporary burdens of racism.

Caretaking Whites: "We Can Choose to Educate Them"

A second theme in the race lessons was that of "caretaking" Whites, or shepherding Whites through various racial events and their racial stupidity at the emotional well-being of people of color. Sometimes the parents instructed the TRAs to take care of the offenders, and sometimes they wanted them to take care of third parties who had witnessed racial events. Caretaking can be viewed as an extension of what bell hooks calls the "servant/served paradigm" (1995, 221). Historically, people of color in the American South were caretakers of Whites, sometimes portrayed in the role of mammy (Hill Collins 2000). The message conveyed to TRAs by several of the adoptive parents' race lessons was that the appropriate and responsible reaction to incidents of racial mistreatment was to suppress and emotionally manage their own feelings in order to serve the needs of Whites. During the interviews, caretaking lessons were often defined and illustrated through incidents of race-based mistreatment against TRAs. Two of the epigraphs from the beginning of the chapter—Ms. Hansen's discussion of hair and Ms. March's exploration of intentions—serve as typical examples of how racial mistreatment generated the delivery of a caretaking race lesson. These responses to racial incidents exemplify the adoptive parents' lessons that focus on educating the offending Whites in order to minimize the future consequences of racial mistreatment for their adoptive children. While the parents' responses demonstrate that the White actors are racially ignorant, the emotional needs of the children are not met. Furthermore, the child is expected to evaluate the severity of the racial incident and the intent of the actor before deciding on a strategy for a cogent response. This places a heavy burden on young, adopted children of color who are essentially on exhibit for Whites to observe and learn about.

By framing racial incidents of mistreatment as interpersonal misunderstandings, the adoptive parents assume White ignorance and normalize their adopted children as exotic and outside of Whiteness. The United States, along with many other countries, has a long history of expecting victims to teach perpetrators about the consequences of racism. As Audre Lorde (1984, 113) notes, "This is an old and primary tool of all oppressors to keep the oppressed occupied with the master's concerns."

During the interviews, the adoptive parents repeatedly presented White racial ignorance as a phenomenon that requires caretaking by African Americans. Mr. Collins related an incident in which his daughter took responsibility for teaching a White family about proper racial etiquette:

> When [my daughter] was in first grade, some girls were screaming across the parking lot the "N word," and that really bothered [her]. And she came back home . . . she was either in first grade or kindergarten . . . and she came in and said, "Dad, I'm going by [a neighbor's] house," and [the neighbor] lived about three houses up. And she came back about fifteen minutes later. Then about fifteen minutes later, we get a knock on the door. And this little kid's standing there, probably about two or three years older than my daughter. And she's bawling, and her folks are standing there. What [my daughter] had done is, she . . . went up there and knocked on the door and got ahold of the mom and said, "Your daughter's calling me the 'N word,' and I think you better do something about it."

She did this without her father knowing. Clearly, the father, or others, had educated her previously about race and racism. She was an assertive young preteenager. Still, the burden to educate the White family was on the daughter. She responded to the incident with literally no adult support, assistance, or supervision despite her young age. She was not given the privilege of racial innocence or ignorance that the White child and the White adults were. Again, assumptions of White innocence guided the interaction.

This is not to say that parents did not take action once they became aware of the problems. Consider the account of Jamal: He had been called the "N word" several times. The "N word" was being used as a term of endearment by some students who considered Jamal to be their friend, but Jamal did not like it. He'd eventually transfer to another high school to escape the name calling. The main issue here is that Jamal's father initially did not know the extent of the problem. Once he found out, he was more than willing to confront the principal of the school and, indirectly, the students. Jamal explained:

> Some ignorant kids just think they're cool. They don't know. Start calling names. Either people just don't do anything about it, or they get their teeth knocked out. Just some kids just thought they were cool, probably didn't know any better. I don't think it was like a malicious attempt, it was just like an ignorant—people asked me, saying, "Hey, do you have a problem with people calling you . . . ?" I was like, "Yeah." And, like, people walked up to me and asked, "What if [I say (the "N word")]?" and I'd say, "I'd hit you." And even girls would ask me, and I'm like, "Yeah, I'd hit 'em. You're lucky you're a girl." A couple kids kept on doing it, so I thought, "I've got to do something about this." So I told my dad, and we just went and saw the principal, and we gave it to him and told him, "My son's gotta get out of the school, or you've got to do something about this right now." So the principal wrote a letter and had the teachers read it. Then after that everyone was like, "I'm so sorry I said this," and I was like, "All right."

Often, however, the adoptee does not have the skills to confront and educate the perpetrator about racism, let alone cope with the incident, and some parents honestly realize their inadequacies. In an attempt to solicit knowledge about race and racial issues for themselves and the adoptees, as well as providing a role model, many of the parents recruited adults from the African American community. Sometimes those recruited were friends or acquaintances of the family, and at other times they were strangers randomly encountered in public places. Consider two accounts from two different White parents. The first is Ms. Hansen's story, quoted in chapter 5, about approaching a Black woman in a restaurant. The second is this account from Ms. White:

> [M]y son was listening to rap music, when every other word was *pussy*, and I said no. He said, "No, Mom, you don't understand; you're White." [An Afri-

can American man] came and taught and said, "No. It has nothing to do with Whites. You don't treat girls and women like that." I've always called on Black people to help me. And they're incredible. Because my kids say, "Oh, it's not just because our mom is White; this is a standard that people have, Black or White."

These adoptive parents acknowledged that African Americans had a unique knowledge about race that they did not have—knowledge that they needed to effectively raise a Black child. These vignettes further exemplify the caretaking of Whites by African Americans, caretaking that was directed at the White adoptive parents themselves this time.

In general, a White racial frame of ignorance was at the center of the adoptive parents' caretaking race lessons. Even African American parents have historically found it necessary to teach children to suppress their own interests and needs to caretake Whites. At one point in time in our nation's history, African Americans could not directly look White folks in the eye and had to move off the sidewalk if a White person was approaching. Subsequently, Black parents taught their children the same lessons in order to literally keep them alive. Dire consequences emerged when those lessons were not followed, as in the case of Emmett Till, who was brutally beaten beyond recognition and tortured by having his eye gouged out, before being shot in the head and tossed into the river, for allegedly whistling at a White woman (Crowe 2002). As Lorde (1984, 75) states, "For survival, black children in America must be raised to be warriors. For survival, they must also be raised to recognize the enemy's many faces." Nowadays, much of the caretaking is in the form of educating Whites on matters of race.

Getting Along with Whites: Have a Peaceful Heart

A third theme evident in the adoptive parents' responses involves the responsibility of transracial adoptees for getting along with, and maintaining harmony with, Whites. Overt conflicts and displays of anger and other negative emotions directed toward Whites were framed as bad and as things to be avoided. As Ms. March instructed, "Don't take offense when there is no offense intended. . . . Change won't come unless you do it with a peaceful heart because people don't want to listen; it's scary for them when you're really angry and militant."

The adoptees were instructed to be calm, conciliatory, nonemotional, and concerned with accommodating the psychological comfort and well-being of Whites. As Ms. March further instructed, "You gain more anger when you give out anger, and you get back what you give, so if you can do it from a peaceful heart and trust that all people really want to be good, and that all people . . . intrinsically can see truth, that's the way I handle it." Even a White sibling named Mason counseled his Black sister, Shante, explaining that "I'm just trying to teach her to open her eyes and look past [the racial incident] when racism came in."

Negative criticism or feedback from the adoptees was regularly silenced as an unreasonable and illegitimate attack on the basic goodness of others, who in these cases were individual Whites. Recall Ms. White's story from chapter 3, about her son saying he hated all Whites aside from her. The lesson Ms. White taught was a noble one: there are some good and some bad White people and, likewise, there are some good and some bad Black people, with most being good. Nevertheless, since the TRAs were surrounded almost exclusively by White people, the lesson taught was that the TRAs were to get along with Whites; resentment toward all the "wonderful White people" her son knew, despite the bad experiences he had, was not considered appropriate or acceptable behavior. At the same time, the parent was quick to point out the suspect actions and character of one "pond-scum Black guy." In essence, the goodness of Whiteness prevails, while the actions of a member of the adoptee's own racial group is used as the bad example. Further, the onus of responsibility for coping with racism is placed on the child.

The consequences of not getting along with Whites were potentially more serious for TRAs than the White family members. To respond negatively to incidents of racial mistreatment was, for the TRA, to risk becoming the stereotypical angry Black male or female. The adoptees may not have understood the consequences of their anger typecasting them as irrational, but the underlying inadvertent message the parents gave, that of controlling one's anger and emotion in order to mollify Whites, fed into the stereotype. Furthermore, the parents' message did not address the seriousness of the event, which was less about emotion and more about power relations.

Still another account by a parent suggests that Black anger was consistently framed and interpreted by the adoptive parents and other Whites as a negative, potentially violent and dangerous force:

> *Ms. Brown:* I have another [African American] daughter that was raised in a very racist black home for ten years, and she—
>
> *Darron:* Racists towards . . . ?
>
> *Ms. Brown:* Whites. Very much; whites were to be used. The only good thing about Whites was their money. She started being very abusive. I mean, it got

> to physical abuse on one of my White daughters, so she [the Black daughter] was placed in [a] treatment center. Well, she was hospitalized for about a week [in the] treatment center and [received] day treatment, and she [the White daughter] still struggles with that.

Recounted as an apparent incident of reverse racism, the adopted Black child was hospitalized presumably for necessary personal work on her dislike toward Whites. Ms. Brown further noted that her Black daughter had acquired a new White friend, and that therefore the rehabilitation process appeared to have been successful in "curing" the child of her racism against White people.

Though hospitalization is an extreme case, the incident reiterates the White racial framing of race as an individual and psychological affair relegated to interpersonal relations. Ironically, the parent continued to articulate the incident from a White perspective.

> *Darron:* That is interesting, given that she is in an all-White family.
>
> *Ms. Brown:* Well, we're not all White, though. Whites are a minority in our family, so you can't really go there.

By pointing to Whites as the numerical minority in their family, she ignores the pervasiveness of Whiteness in the larger society. Even though demographers maintain that America is becoming more diverse and less White, this does not mean that people of color will suddenly ascend to higher status and power. Recall the experiences in South Africa during the height of apartheid, where the numerical majority of that nation was indigenous African, as compared to the descendants of Dutch Afrikaners who settled the region in the 1600s. The Dutch descendants controlled every facet of the country, including the establishment of shantytowns still in existence.

Reverse racism is a contemporary concept that is increasingly invoked within dominant U.S. society to absolve Whites of systematic exploitation and racism. Many Whites claim that African Americans are at times just as racist as Whites, and even worse at times. However, the concept of reverse racism ignores the structural and systemic realities of White racism. As we have maintained throughout this book, racism is a system of unearned privileges that benefits the dominant group at the expense of others.

The adoptive parents generally recognized frequent instances of racial mistreatment against TRAs, especially at school. And when instances occurred, they were prompt at intervention. The parents frequently reported ongoing racial discrimination and abuse of their adopted children. Often the school and district personnel were unresponsive unless the parents persisted and insisted that something be done. Thus, ironically, the parents' awareness of racial mistreatment against their TRAs tended to buttress the White racial frame of White goodness while undermining the consequences of racial mistreatment for the adopted children. In other words, racial events became about the parents' needs rather than about teaching, trying to help their children understand race, and protecting identities. The adoptive parents were regularly accused of reverse racism, exaggeration, overreacting, and "playing the race card." One White parent, Ms. Ross, reported: "So one time I went in to the teacher and I said, 'I'm trying to understand what's going on here.' And she said, 'Don't you pull a race card with me.'" In response, Ms. Ross spent immense time, energy, emotion, and perseverance in attempting to redress the situation and protect her adopted son from the harmful consequences of the racial mistreatment. As the following racial events demonstrate, even in the midst of their struggles against racial mistreatment, the adoptive parents nevertheless still insisted on the racial frame of White goodness and racial innocence:

> *Mr. Stevens:* And a group of kids in a car yelled out the window, the "N word," you know. But you have to, you know, kick yourself in the pants and say, "Hey guys, you know the world's full of bigots and people that are ignorant." And then you just have to . . . well . . . there's a time to step up and say and do something. 'Cause I had to get in the principal's face . . . and he's a nice guy, and they're all nice guys, and I didn't take it personally, but there are times when I had to stand up. I had to say, "Guys, this is unacceptable," that kind of thing.

Likewise, Ms. Ross reported,

> Within an hour, I had a meeting with district people, and those boys were removed from the classroom. But if I really thought that color didn't matter, would I have said, "Okay, that's all right, yeah, he'll move to this other classroom; we don't want to cause any trouble"? . . . I didn't. I mean, I can still talk to this woman. I have [a large family]; I don't burn bridges, and there's a way to be respectful but still be firm in what you're expectation is for your child. And she came around and she, at the end, actually was crying in her own office and apologizing for her behavior.

While Ms. Ross didn't "pull the race card," the interaction makes it clear that the school-district people were trying to minimize the incident's racial significance.

Using the White racial frame to make sense of racial mistreatment, the adoptive parents maintained the innocence and goodness of Whites as they worked to minimize or avoid conflict and get along with other Whites. With the adoptive parents insisting on the sanctity of White goodness and racial innocence, the injury inflicted by these racial incidents became almost incidental. As one parent reported, "Personally, I can still talk to this woman." By framing the event as a personal momentary failing, she can avoid framing the incident as racial. But by doing so, she minimizes the consequences of racial mistreatment in order to get along with Whites.

Black folks do (still) have to get along with White folks, and Whites often (still) do not have to get along with Blacks. As James Cone (2004, 144) says, "The quality of white life is hardly ever affected by what blacks think and do. However, everything whites think and do impacts profoundly on the lives of blacks on a daily basis. We can never escape white power and its cruelty."

Get Your Black Culture

In this chapter we have examined three themes of cultural-socialization practices of White adoptive parents of Black children. Each of the three themes carries a specific understanding or interpretation of race, and how the adoptive parents teach TRAs constitutes a lesson about how to contend with, cope with, and counter racism. Specifically, the adoptive parents' race lessons emphasize the TRAs' racial background and culture as an individual possession and a special knowledge about race not held by Whites. These patterns of understanding race were made concrete through the adoptive parents' cultural-socialization practices as race lessons, in teaching TRAs to (1) affirm and feel positively about racial differences; (2) subvert personal feelings and responses to racial mistreatment, to help Whites learn about race and racism; and (3) develop a thick skin to deflect the consequences of mistreatment in a way that avoids conflict and does not disrupt harmony with Whites.

In many ways, the adoptive parents were willing to challenge the colorblind perspective that many Whites hold. The parents acknowledged matters of race and racism, rather than denying them. Using color-conscious race lessons, the adoptive parents taught TRAs both to affirm race and to combat racism by celebrating racial differences, by caretaking, and by getting along with Whites.

A major effect of the adoptive parents' color-conscious race lessons was to infuse race into the identity development of TRAs. A strong and positive sense of self-worth and the ability to competently rise above and deflect threats to the self are important components of resiliency (Hill 1998; Kunjufu 1995; Pollack 2005). Resiliency is a protective mechanism that is requisite for individuals to successfully struggle against racism (Hall 2007; Phinney et al. 1997). In many ways, the adoptive parents' race lessons reflected those lessons conveyed by Black parents. Both adoptive parents and African American parents have also been concerned that their children feel good about themselves and affirm their racial background. Similarly, both the adoptive parents and Black parents traditionally provide "the child criteria for determining malice" when faced with racism, and help "the child determine what action was then appropriate for retribution or redistribution" (Ward 1990, 223).

When reinterpreted through distinctively Black traditions and collective experiences, however, the adoptive parents' race lessons contrasted markedly with those of African American parents. To celebrate racial differences and to caretake and get along with Whites, from the adoptive parents' perspective, meant teaching TRAs to accept the privileging of White characteristics and assumptions of White racial innocence and ignorance. The race lessons taught the adopted children of color to think about race in the way that Whites do—that is, with Whiteness considered as normal. Repeatedly, the adoptees were taught that White people are virtuous and good people who just don't know a lot about race—but they can be taught.

As articulated by the adoptive parents, the three race lessons were characterized by a decidedly liberal-humanist approach to race that strongly privileges the individual and culture as private property (Bonilla-Silva 2003; Dawson 1994). Reinterpreted through African American traditions, the three race lessons take on a very different meaning. In the Black community, the emphasis is much more on the community rather than the individual (Dawson 1994; Foner 1999). Cultural pride, framed by African American traditions, was not something to be possessed by the individual, but something that accrued to the individual as part of a collective struggle for racial-group uplift (Barkley Brown 1994; Gaines 1996). Indeed, individual African Americans taking positions perceived to harm the Black community continue to be "considered traitors, stripped of community-derived benefits and publicly condemned and humiliated" (Dawson 1994, 203).

The parents we interviewed had immense and deep parental love for their adopted children, and they had antiracist intentions. The parents' emphasis on White frameworks in the race lessons emerged when viewed through the distinctively African American cultural values, collective achievements, and historical experiences. The privileging of the individual and the assumption of White racial innocence reflected the Whiteness of the adoptive parents' own experience with race. Because they interpreted race events through their own perspectives, the adoptive parents' race lessons recentered and recreated the White racial frame, at the same time that they failed to disturb the existing racial hierarchy.

The adoptive parents' three race lessons were drawn from the larger historical patterns and the ways that Whites have interpreted issues of race. Individualism, meritocracy, and assumptions of White goodness have shaped, guided, and validated White subjugation of African Americans and people of color from the nation's founding (Lipsitz 2006). Embedded within the race lessons we have examined here, assumptions of Whiteness and possessive individualism connected the adoptive parents to these historical patterns of thinking about race and to the existing racial hierarchy.

CHAPTER SEVEN

Addressing Race with Your Children

Practical Advice for White Adoptive Parents

IN THIS final chapter, we offer some conclusions to our research and scholarship. As researchers and writers on race and ethnic relations, we have each had long commitments to making the world a better place, a place in which race no longer matters. Sadly, as we have researched transracial adoption we have come to realize all the more that racism remains a part of American life. We begin this chapter with the personal voice and sentiments of the first author, Darron Smith, as he articulates the challenges he faces in rearing his two biracial daughters in our dominant White society.

Darron Smith's Story

I am an African American man entrusted with raising two biracial daughters who, like me, are situated within U.S. society with its avoidance of its racial past. Many pieces of wisdom were passed down to me from the strong Black women who raised me, advice that taught me how to nurture my own daughters to be confident, productive Black women in our society. Yet I still have the challenge of guiding them through a White world and, in particular, the challenge of doing so in the predominantly White community where they live.

The adoptive parents we worked with as part of this study were not at all reticent to talk to me as a Black man about their efforts to raise Black children—indeed, they sometimes seemed almost overly eager to know my thoughts on how to best raise Black and biracial adoptive children. Many of the conversations with the parents would occur before the actual interviews began. Wanting to establish rapport with the parents, I frequently made mention of my own two daughters. As we would talk about some of our shared challenges in raising Black children, the adoptive parents often wanted me to provide them with particular parenting strategies for teaching their children how to contend with racism. The parents tended to assume that as a researcher and Black father, I might have the answers. In fact, I found myself having to temper my desire to shake some sense into some of them as I heard repeated stories of missed opportunities. However, because I was one of the researchers on this project, I was in their homes to find out what they did to raise their Black children—not to tell them how I raise my own Black children. Hence, I did not feel the liberty at the time to share any of my own insights as a parent.

I now take the opportunity to share some of the thoughts and responses that I wanted to share with the parents then. More specifically, I will reflect on some of my experiences raising my daughters and discussing race and racial matters with White adoptive parents. By no means do I feel that I am a better parent than any of the adoptive parents in our study, or any other parent, for that matter—nor do I have all the answers in child rearing. However, having been a Black child growing up in the South when race was still quite volatile,[1] and being now a Black parent in racially White Utah, I have gained great insights with the specific task of raising Black children to be "warriors," full of confidence and a no-nonsense approach to engaging racism. It is my sincere wish that these ideas be of some benefit to the many White families in U.S. society who are adopting children across historical boundaries of race.

Black Identity and Stereotypes

My colleagues and I had the pleasure of discussing many important issues related to transracial adoption. At times, I had to hold back my emotions as I listened to these brave parents and adult adoptees open their world to complete strangers. I was physically and emotionally drained after many of the interview sessions. In many of the interviews we conducted, I was stunned by the adoptees' beliefs and how they, with no apparent awareness, reinforced the stereotypically negative views of African Americans as represented in the media. It almost appeared as if during the interview process the adoptees forgot that I was also a Black man, because many of them shared their ideas of Blacks as lazy, ugly, oversexed, and violent, thus subjecting me to various forms of stereotypical portrayals of Blacks and biases against Blacks. I worried that their ideas constituted a form of Black self-hatred as evidenced through their countless stories. For example, one biracial adoptee articulated that she did not believe Black men were attractive. She had never dated a Black man and just felt more comfortable dating White men. Notably, she simultaneously conceded that she did not get asked out on dates that often, and the young woman had an idea that being Black was a limiting factor. Another adoptee said that her adoptive parents did not want her dating Black men. When I asked why her parents felt that way, she explained that her parents believed many of the invidious stereotypes so commonly represented in U.S society. The degree of Black demonization exemplified by many of the adoptees was evident to me, and I could see why so many struggle with identity issues.

My Children and Race Issues

Reflecting on these experiences, I found myself swept away thinking about my own daughters and what they would likely encounter while growing up in a predominately White community. I am without a set of eyes and ears regarding the daily happenings in the lives of my girls when they are not in my care. I must rely on my children to tell their stories about what is happening in their lives. I am not surprised that my girls have encountered many of the same race-based issues as the adoptees. After all, my children could easily be mistaken for transracially adopted children given the dearth of racial diversity in their community. They represent a mere handful of children of color in the White suburban school they attend. I have witnessed a few other (monoracial) Black children roaming the hallways on occasion during my visits. Indeed they were each adopted, presumably by White families. These Black and biracial children, including my own girls, living in a predominately White society and being raised by White parents in a White family, tend to view the world through the prism of Whiteness; but they still remain visibly a part of the Black world. This constitutes a paradox for these adoptees, a cultural mismatch that I believe carries over into their adult lives. For the White parents to be unclear on the question of race and its role in the lives of their children, and to feel that discussing racial matters causes their children to needlessly dwell on the topic, does not help in the development of a positive racial identity. Just the opposite would be true. Engage children, help them reframe ignorant questions, and teach them how to unlearn the very racial issues that are a source of identity confusion and frustration.

The reality of these conversations and observations led me to reflect on the need to constantly devise ways to disrupt racism and to inoculate my own daughters in healthy and meaningful ways. Leaving children without the means to psychologically protect themselves is akin to allowing a school bully to pointlessly harass a child without any recourse. Thus, teaching my girls to be aware of and responsive to race-based mistreatment became one of the many important lessons I learned through the process of listening to White adoptive parents speak their truth. In other words, I wanted to turn the tables back on White people, causing them to observe and think about the questions, actions, and statements they make regarding race and difference. I have used the technique of restating a question applied in the college classroom when teaching White students about a difficult racial topic. As someone who teaches complex subject matter on race, I know that reframing a question when its smacks of gross insensitivity, even when not intended, is a great way to create a dialogue and educate others.

For example, I have heard many stories from my children and the adoptees themselves about White children being fascinated with Black hair. The White children cannot seem to stop touching and feeling the tresses of Black hair: pulling the hair and swirling the kinky locks between their White fingers are common occurrences. Even skin color is a source of great amusement for White children unaccustomed to Black people. I recall a time from my own experience when I attended a small liberal-arts college in Idaho. I stayed with a White family a few weeks before fall semester began. I had the youngest brother of my friend, a six-year-old, unexpectedly hop in my lap and proceed to rub my skin while enunciating "Does it come off, Darron?" I was taken aback by this seemingly innocent gesture that left me with deep feelings of insecurity about myself as a young Black man at the time. Was the difference that striking? I reasoned in my head. Despite the conversations I'd had all my life with family members about race, I must say I was unprepared to fully respond to this young child. I was simply at a loss for words. One of the race lessons passed down by my maternal grandmother was to address directly White ignorance in race matters. Thus, when a White person

> wants to feel your hair, you retort with, "Why don't you touch [your White friend]'s hair?" Or when a White person is fascinated by the color of your skin, ask to rub his or her skin. My hope is that parents will be mindful of and act on such innocent racial acts before their children are speechless about how to respond to race events that could potentially scar their fragile identities.
>
> As a result of this project, raising my girls to have a healthy and positive self-concept weighed heavily on my mind. As a father, it is a hard enough challenge making sure my daughters are raised to be focused, self-confident, educated, independent, assertive, and caring women in our society. And as a parent, teaching them about the vicissitudes of race and racism in U.S. society in a manner in which they do not learn to hate White folk, but instead develop the skills to reframe the constant indignities and the assaults on their character, becomes an arduous task.

Throughout this book, we have discussed many of the experiences the adoptive parents shared with us. Their stories and their motivations for adopting across the color line were truly inspiring, and we appreciated very much the struggles that they faced in raising Black children. In this final chapter, we outline a few ideas for parents in preparing their children for the racism and racial mistreatment they will inevitably encounter. The first suggestion is that parents not assume that we are living in a "postracial society." And we hope that parents will feel inclined to implement some of our further suggestions below.

Concerns of Black Child-Care Advocates

Unfortunately, most White parents do not know much about African American racial history, and few have significant friends of color. Thus, Black child-care advocates are afraid that Whites' intentions will actually do more harm than good. The controversy regarding whether White parents should adopt children of color remains an important dialogue for White parents to consider. If they do adopt, White parents must keep in mind that when a laissez-faire approach to Black identity construction is maintained within White households, identity development is compromised. In 1972, the National Association of Black Social Workers (NABSW) issued a strong statement against the transracial adoption of

Black children by White parents. We revisit their statement, quoted at length below, as a way to provide White parents with the concerns of the organization that represents thousands of Black social workers. In providing a rationale for their position, the National Association of Black Social Workers (1972) declared:

> We affirm the inviolable position of Black children in Black families where they belong physically, psychologically, and culturally in order that they receive the total sense of themselves and develop a sound projection of their future. . . . Black children in White homes are cut off from the healthy development of themselves as Black people, which development is the normal expectation and only true humanistic goal. Identity grows on the three levels of all human development: the physical, psychological, and cultural; and the nurturing of self-identity is a prime function of the family. The incongruence of a White family performing this function for a Black child is easily recognized. The physical factor stands to maintain that child's difference from his [or her] family. There is no chance of his [or her] resembling any relative. One's physical identity with his [or her] own kind is of great significance. . . . In our society, the developmental needs of Black children are significantly different from those of White children. Black children are taught, from an early age, highly sophisticated coping techniques to deal with racist practices perpetrated by individuals and institutions. . . . Only a Black family can transmit the emotional and sensitive subtleties of perception and reaction essential for a Black child's survival in a racist society. Our society is distinctly Black or White and characterized by White racism at every level. We repudiate the fallacious and fantasized reasoning of some that Whites adopting Black children will alter that basic character.

Following their 1972 statement, the NABSW put forth two main arguments and took a stance against transracial adoption, arguing that it is not in the best interests of Black children. First, transracial adoption, they argued, is not in the interests of Black children because adoptees raised in White homes are not likely to develop a positive Black racial identity and may likely lose their culture in the process. Second, transracial adoption separates Black children from Black communities, and the collective memory and racial knowledge about living with racism handed down over generations is lost. The NABSW has since modified its position, in part, because of the large number of Black children in the foster-care system. They modified their position to argue that, in circumstances where Black families are unavailable, White families can be a viable alternative. Their position, however, is that transracial adoption should be considered a last resort as opposed to a first choice. Clearly, we would rather see more children adopted than have them wade through the bureaucracy of foster care, regardless of the racial composition of the home. If White parents are going to adopt Black children, however, they must be willing to put in the time and do the work of unlearning White racial frames, preferably before the child becomes a social experiment. Therefore, the choice to transracially adopt is incredibly complex, requiring the consideration of many factors before a decision can be made.

Taking Action: Key Recommendations for Parent Involvement

Given the overwhelming presence of racism in U.S. society, what can White adoptive parents do to better ensure a happy, healthy, and positive experience for their transracially adopted child? Here we suggest some additional strategies that we have seen transracial families in our study successfully implement. First, White adoptive parents rearing Black adoptees must be proactive in the process of understanding the unique circumstances faced by their adoptive children. We encourage parents to model appropriate behavior for their children by living their lives in ways that foster openness and genuine honesty about race differences rather than colorblind disingenuousness. It is not enough to sit on the sidelines or maintain a distance as a "project manager" when it comes to unlearning the White racial-socialization practices that contribute to children feeling inadequately prepared to address racial issues. Parents must become engaged. Denying, minimizing, or invoking individualism as a plausible explanation for race-based mistreatment is not especially helpful considering the evidence we have presented in this book. Sensitivity to racial mistreatment, dialogues about it, involvement with the adoptee's birth community, and a search for models from that community are critical to avoid feelings of low self-esteem, depression, acting out, and identity confusion. These negative consequences are not automatic; however, we are merely saying be mindful of and attentive to race and racism, and how Whiteness structures the lives of transracial adoptees. This issue cannot be overstated, particularly when White people in general remain mystified by and angry over the insistence by people of color that racism remains the elephant in the room.

We strongly recommend that White adoptive parents take courses on racism, such as "Racism 101," to better prepare themselves for the community they are joining and to be accountable for their Black children. Such courses are not readily apparent but can be sought out at local community colleges and universities. Ethnic-studies, social-work, and African American–studies departments are excellent places to explore potential courses, and sometimes adoption agencies offer cursory seminars on what White parents can do. A few of our respondents did immerse themselves in this undertaking. Others, however, were oblivious to the consequences they would bring about by adopting transracially. Children of color deserve reassurance from their adoptive parents that they will provide them not only with much-needed love, but also with proper training and schooling in the four-hundred-year-old problem of White racism. To begin with, White parents and all of their children must start reading fiction and nonfiction books by Black authors. Listed below are a few such books that we recommend:

Afro Bets Book of Black Heroes from A to Z, by Wade Hudson and Valerie Wilson Wesley
Barack Obama: Son of Promise, Child of Hope, by Nikki Grimes
Forty Acres and Maybe a Mule, by Harriette Gillem Robinet
Girls Hold Up This World, by Jada Pinkett Smith
I Like Myself! by Karen Beaumont
I Love My Hair! by Natasha Anastasia Tarpley
My America, by Jan Spivey Gilchrist
Of Thee I Sing: A Letter to My Daughters, by Barack Obama
Shanna's Doctor Show, by Jean Marzollo

We argue that reading with adopted children of color is key to improving their understanding of Black Americans' long engagement with White society. It is one way to instill a sense of Black pride that helps buttress racial identity. Black history can be the fulcrum for this endeavor. The accomplishments of Dr. Martin Luther King, Jr., Rosa Parks, and Jackie Robinson, for example, are good places to start for parents. However, White adoptive parents must not sanitize Black history and marginalize its importance. Many of the adoptive parents made clear that reading books was an important aspect of their time with their children. We encourage the parents, however, to go deeper in understanding the Black freedom struggle or collective historical experience for the sake of their children. Discuss the content of these books, particularly the nonfiction books. Discussion can take place between parent and parent, between parent and child, and even between parents and their White and non-White friends. Do not gloss over White racism in our American history as merely "just slavery," something that happened in the past. Racism is far more subtle today, but just as damaging to African Americans and other Americans of color.

Since formal education is also significantly lacking in its ability to deliver on the promises made to students of color, parents must augment their child's educational experiences. Public education and universities are saturated with Eurocentric curriculum, which leaves significant gaps in our history and glorifies Whiteness at the expense of people of color and their contributions. Parents must be aware of this slant to public education and become proactive and even vigilant with regard to the need to supplement the instruction to adequately represent the interests of the oppressed peoples. The onus is on the White parents to become students of Black history, so that when lessons are extracted from the pages of significant books, parents can speak from an educated point of view. These parents can teach their children about the contributions made by Black Americans who paid a heavy price for the freedoms we all now enjoy. Becoming a student of Black history is to become a student of American history.

In order for White parents to disrupt stereotypes about Black people, research on racial stereotyping suggests that White Americans must have significant interactions with people of color of equal status (Jackman 1996). Rather than merely having casual acquaintances who are Black, parents must expand their circle of friends to include those of color, and be equally vested in inviting them into their personal space to engage in fellowship as they would their White friends. Likewise, parents need to create those same opportunities for their children. Whenever possible, families must seek to live in a diverse community and participate in Black-centered activities.

Just as intellectual stimulation and engagement are important for developing a positive Black identity, activities of daily living such as hair and skin care promote a healthy self-concept for Black children. Hair is a very important component of self-esteem because, from very early on, it carries many messages about one's "coolness" factor and is tied to peer-group popularity. Therefore, parents should not only take their children to Black hair salons and barbers but also become proficient in doing Black hair themselves, and they should understand the significance of hair in the Black community. As we saw in our interviews, several parents had to learn to take care of their children's hair, and still many did not even attempt the task. The act of doing your child's hair shows interest in him or her as an individual and provides a great bonding opportunity for parent and child. Likewise, skin care is another important dimension of knowing what children of color need. Black skin requires attention. A "wash and wear" approach to skin is not helpful, especially when Black and biracial children are prone to skin allergies. For example, parents must ensure that Black adoptees wear alcohol-free lotion and emollients, to minimize the potential manifestations of allergies in the form of skin rashes and itching. In the Black community, being seen as "ashy" or having dry skin can be a form of hazing and taunting by peers. Keeping children properly lubricated reduces the propensity toward allergies and helps maintain a healthy sense of self and Black identity.

Other approaches to consider for White adoptive parent involvement in a child's racial well-being involve contact with, and the forging of strong relationships with, extended-family members or birth parents wherever possible. We feel it is in the best interests of the child if the White parents can maintain contact. Do not assume these extended-family members don't want to be involved; reach out to them. Also, join a support group and use this as a basis to unlearn racism. Finally, understand White privilege, and stop allowing yourself to be easily offended and defensive when faced with the realities of your White perspectives and biases. If these lessons aren't directly linked to ending White supremacy and White privilege, then they are fleeting at best.

At the heart of transracial adoption is the goal of finding good homes and loving parents for thousands of children trapped in a broken and disorganized child-welfare system. The trend of transracial adoption will continue and will likely increase as birth rates for White families continue to decrease. It is imperative that White adoptive parents take concerted action to assume responsibility for their transracial adoptees and unlearn the White norms, attitudes, and beliefs about the human condition that have so long plagued White Americans. In table 7.1, we forecast what could happen if White adoptive families, indeed, all Whites, reenvisioned a world without the constraints of Whiteness.

Imagining New Race Lessons

Audre Lorde (1984, 74) has noted that "[r]aising black children—male and female—in the mouth of a racist, sexist, suicidal dragon is perilous and

Table 7.1. Transition from Whiteness to Progressive Parenting

Race Lessons Grounded in Whiteness: Emphasis on Individualism, Colorblindness, and Idealism	*Race Lessons Reimagined without Whiteness*
Reading a book about Nat Turner as a man who hated slavery and worked to end it and recognizing that Turner's cause was much greater than acts of random violence against innocent Whites	Reading revisionist history, as understood by scholars of color, about the pernicious foundations of American society and learning more about American racial history
Living in culturally homogeneous neighborhoods where a few adoptees of color and upper-middle-class people of color reside, and calling that "free choice" and "progress"	Promoting more Black-owned businesses that serve Black communities
Having acquaintanceships with people of color passed off as "best friends"	Having more significant friends of color who are not merely acquaintances
Recognizing that *individualism* is euphemistic for White separatism, and understanding that "merit" is problematic for communities of color	Listening to the voices of people of color about the racial mistreatment they experience on any particular day, and working toward ending all forms of racial discrimination
Understanding American history as "plain old history" while ignoring the contributions of Native Americans, African Americans, and other Americans of color	Having more African Americans and other Americans of color in prominent positions, where they can effectuate change in ways that attend to the poor, the needy, and the forsaken
Avoiding discussions about race as overly polemical, and Blacks and other people of color as whiners	Engaging in discussions about race and the role that Whiteness plays in maintaining the status quo

chancy." Our analysis of the adoptive parents' race lessons provides an example of White domination even in a realm where the participants intended otherwise. These race lessons reveal how systemic and seductive racist practices may exist in the home and channel the experiences of individuals and families toward reproducing the racial structure.

One alternative for reframing the adoptive parents' race lessons is to do so through the traditions of the African American experience. Another is to disconnect Whiteness and the existing White racial privilege. According to James Baldwin (1980, 1),

> To be black [is] to confront, and to be forced to alter, a condition forged in history. To be white [is] to be forced to digest a delusion called white supremacy.

> Indeed, without confronting the history that has either given white people an identity or divested them of it, it is hardly possible for anyone who thinks of himself as white to know what a black person is talking about at all.

Consequently, reinterpretations of the adoptive parents' race lessons through the prism of the Black experience may provide a useful space for (re)imagining race lessons from a more democratic center, ones that learn from the historical experiences of racial minorities within the context of White supremacy. Most importantly, learning from the historical experiences of African Americans means re-creating the adoptive parents' race lessons in ways that eradicate the Whiteness embedded within them.

From the position of the "faces at the bottom of the well" (Bell 1992), the historical struggle of African Americans against racism "opens up political possibilities unimaginable to those tethered to the white world" (Olson 2004, 133). As Malcolm X once declared, "We have to keep in mind at all times that we are not fighting for integration, nor are we fighting for separation. We are fighting for recognition as human beings. We are fighting for the right to live as free humans in this society. In fact, we are actually fighting for rights that are even greater than civil rights and that is [*sic*] human rights."[2]

Accordingly, parents who adopt transracially need to be careful what race lessons they teach. They must sensitize their TRAs about "the 'politicization' of everyday life" (Foner 1990, 53); they must learn to think about and understand race through Black experiences. Cultural socialization and racial inculcation are not processes of what to do with racial differences; they are processes of how to think and how to interpret the surrounding world in ways that challenge and are not dependent on the Whiteness of liberal-humanism traditions. By thinking differently about race, the adoptive parents (and the rest of us) learn how to act in more democratic and inclusive ways based on the full personhood of all people, rather than on the privileging of Whiteness. As Maya Angelou (1993) says, "I speak to the black experience, but I am always talking to the human condition."

Summary and Conclusion

As Richard Wright (1957) intimated in his work on race relations, most White people know exactly what needs to be done to resolve what he referred to as "the white problem" in the Western world, but would rather die than do it. Parents must be willing to take proactive and corrective measures that ensure the success of their children; otherwise, adoptions across the color line are nothing more than bodies occupying space. The unique circumstances of transracial adoptions require special insights and provisions. The question is whether or not White parents will step forward in the interest of teaching their children of color a "loving ethic" that is rooted in racial understanding and confidence. We remain hopeful that White adoptive parents and society in general can and will answer this most pressing call. In these circumstances, love is not enough.

APPENDIX A

A Note about Our Methods and Methodology

AS THE reader knows, this book is about the often poignant stories of parents and children from transracially adoptive families. The stories are both powerful and important because they reflect and relay a richness of meanings and knowledge derived from the teller's lived experiences and realities. Individuals, as we mention in the text, use these meanings to make sense of and act on the world around them. Exploring the stories individuals tell about their lives helps us to uncover and examine the meanings that are important in the storyteller's life.

For interested readers, we discuss the methods we used and how we went about collecting the stories that we used for this book's study. Our purpose here is to briefly define for the reader what *qualitative research* is and describe its main characteristics, since we used a qualitative methodology. We want to help readers understand why we chose qualitative-research methods for this study, and how we have used a qualitative methodology to help us explore and make sense of transracial adoption and its many dimensions.

The Stories We Tell about Our Lives

When people talk about their lives, they usually tell stories. The subject matter of stories is human activity. The respondents who participated in this study, by recounting and discussing their experiences as members of transracially adoptive families, constructed and shared stories of action and activity that had meaning for them. These stories display the ways individuals understand the relationships between and consequences of events in their lives.

Examining participants' stories allows us to identify and examine the salient meanings within TRA families. Stories "express a kind of knowledge that uniquely describes human experience in that actions and happenings contribute positively and negatively to attaining goals and fulfilling purposes" (Polkinghorne 1995, 8). Stories are important because they outline why actions were taken and what the results were. Stories, moreover, are powerful because they evoke emotions and transform both listeners of stories and the storytellers themselves.

Gathering Stories Using Qualitative Research

The stories we use come from in-depth interviews we conducted with both transracial adoptees, who are now adults, and parents who had adopted transracially. This form of data collection, known as qualitative research, can be described as research that is focused on meaning but also meaning making. Qualitative research is an examination of actions and words that produce meaning. It is "verbal and visual rather than statistical" (Morrow and Smith 2000, 199). It is grounded in the details and descriptive narratives of people's lives. Put simply, qualitative research is research that asks, "How do people make sense of their lives?"

The role of the researcher in this type of research is to capture and interpret the complexities of the social world being studied (Denzin and Lincoln 2000; Merriam 2001). In qualitative research, the researcher becomes the instrument, a partner who shares the lives and experiences of the respondents. The interviews enable the researchers to examine recurring patterns of actions and words salient to the lives of the individuals (Angrosina and Mays de Perez 2000; Fontana and Frey 2000; Kvale 1996).

The reader can see this involvement of the researchers in the interview excerpts we discuss throughout the book. All meanings are mediated by and through the researcher's own experiences and social position with regard to race, socioeconomic class, religion, gender, and other markers of social differences. As researchers conduct interviews and study the lives of other people, they too are making sense of stories through the stories of their own lives. Indeed, the researcher learns about herself or himself by studying other people (Fine 1994; Gitlin 1990).

The meanings conveyed within stories reflect and emerge from a particular social context (Dei and Johal 2005; Reinharz 1992). The interviews we conducted were open ended and free-flowing. They allowed meanings to emerge. We were not asking questions for which we were looking for a particular answer. We wanted the answers to come from what the adoptive parents and adoptees knew from their lived experiences, not what we hoped or wanted to hear. As researchers, we had to continually work back and forth between generating meanings by asking open-ended questions and then testing those meanings for salience among study participants by asking the people we interviewed if we correctly understood what meanings they were trying to convey to us (see Coffey and Atkinson 1996; Patton 1990).

The open-ended dimension of qualitative research allowed us to explore the experiences, motives, and outcomes of the transracial-adoption experience. Through the process of raising adopted Black children, White parents daily create, negotiate, and act on the meanings of race and racism. These meanings profoundly influence both parents and children. We wanted to know what those meanings were, and we didn't know what meanings individuals would share with us during the interviews.

The open-ended dimension of qualitative research also infers a constructivist-interpretivist perspective. From this perspective, the hopes, expectations, feelings, and aspirations of both the researchers and the respondents guide the research process; they cannot be separated out from the research process (Ponterotto 2005). All of us consider ourselves to be race scholars who are deeply committed to ending all forms of racism. In the actual interviews, however, we attempted to be value neutral so that the values, life choices, and perspectives of those involved in transracial adoption could come through as they understood them.

Notwithstanding our efforts to be neutral, our views likely leaked through in a variety of ways—through the questions we asked, for example, and the mere fact that we were interviewing the respondents about their perspectives on race and transracial adoption. We attempted, however, to minimize the influence of our own values on the research process and its outcomes (Eisner and Peshkin 1990). One way we attempted to do this was to conduct interviews in pairs. Darron Smith identifies as an African American, and Cardell Jacobson and Brenda Juárez identify as White Americans.

We conducted the interviews together for several reasons. The family members we interviewed were placed in a position of vulnerability because we were asking them to talk about topics that are often seen as taboo in our society—topics of race and racism. We wanted to make sure that the people we interviewed were not unduly subjected to any questions or interactions that would make them feel uncomfortable or threatened.

Hence, we worked first to establish a positive relationship with the respondents. We recognized the risks taken by the respondents as part of their agreement to be interviewed. They were willing to discuss their lives. They understood that their lives were on display in public places. At the same time, the individuals who participated in our study felt that they had an important story to tell. We too felt that they had an important story to tell. To minimize these vulnerabilities and protect the respondents, we worked hard to create an atmosphere of trust, honesty, and respectfulness.

We explained to the respondents that we wanted to understand and present their lives. We felt that using one Black and one White interviewer would help us establish a positive relationship with the respondents, one of equal power and one illustrating Blacks and Whites working together. We did not want the potential for the racial dynamics of a Black interviewer discussing issues of race and racism to cause undue discomfort for any of the White adoptive parents. At the same time, we also felt that the presence of a Black man would help adoptees feel more comfortable during interviews when they were asked to talk about matters of race relations.

As we conducted interviews, we found that the adoptive parents in this study were highly conscious of race and racism. They did not discount the experiences and traditions of African Americans with race and racism. Indeed, many of the adoptive parents seemed to be highly solicitous of Darron as a Black man; they were sincere in welcoming both of us into their homes. They would frequently turn to Darron to ask his opinions about topics we discussed in the interviews. Darron felt that the respondents looked to him as a role model for their children and that they were generally emotionally warm toward him. He sometimes worked hard to reiterate to the adoptive parents that he wanted to know what *they* thought and experienced.

The parents also seemed eager and pleased, not uncomfortable in the least, to share their experiences with us, and particularly with Darron as an African American. The adoptees themselves were likewise very candid and open in sharing their experiences. The younger the adoptees, the more they seemed to struggle, however, to have something to say about race. Yet their hesitation did not seem to me to be based on Darron's identity as a Black man. The older adoptees seemed to be better able to share their narratives and better articulate their feelings about their experiences with racial matters.

With the exception of three interviews, Darron Smith and Cardell Jacobson conducted all of the interviews together, in person. Two interviews from North Carolina and one from Pennsylvania were conducted by telephone. Each interview was recorded and transcribed with the permission of participants. Informed consent forms reiterated that participants' actual names would not be disclosed and that their responses would not jeopardize their standing or status in the community or any other social context; this has been realized.

The remaining interviews were conducted in Utah, a state that is dominated by the Church of Jesus Christ of Latter-day Saints (commonly described as the LDS Church, or the Mormon Church—because of its use of the Book of Mormon as scripture). African Americans constitute roughly 1 percent of the citizens of Utah, though several other minority groups also have a presence in Utah. The low number of African Americans in the state increases the saliency of transracial-adoption issues there. While the LDS Church has a history of racial discrimination, Cardell Jacobson (2004) and Armand Mauss (2004) have shown that Mormon racial attitudes are not significantly different from those of the nation as a whole. Importantly, the small number of African Americans in Utah makes the individuals and family we interviewed unusual. Because they were transracial families, they were often the object of attention in Utah.

We began the interviews by asking them to describe the family and then gradually moved to their experiences and perspectives regarding race, racism, and racial identity. We followed a general protocol, but allowed the interviews to follow the interests and comments of those whom we interviewed. The questions generally focused on the daily lives and life opportunities of adoptees, their adoptive parents, and the family unit. If the respondents did not mention racial incidents, we probed to ascertain their experiences with racism and their reactions. Interviews typically lasted from sixty to ninety minutes.

Selection Procedures and Recruitment

We recruited the participants using a snowball, or *chain*, technique (Patton 1990). But we also used purposeful sampling. The intent of purposeful sampling is to describe and analyze a particular subgroup in depth by selecting participants who maximize or minimize group differences (Strauss and Corbin 1990). The snowball technique allowed us to draw on individual respondents' knowledge of other TRA families. This, in turn, allowed us to identify other potential participants.

All of the adoptive parents and adult adoptees were willing and generous with their time, knowledge, and experiences regarding transracial adoption. As we have noted, they seemed eager to tell their stories, and they were willing to refer us to other participants. In the end we found many more potential participants than we could actually interview.

As with any human experience, those of White parents and Black adoptees are complex; the experiences don't come in any particular order. They are necessarily multilayered (Polkinghorne 2005). No one data source can adequately capture the richness, depth, and complexity of any human condition (Morrow and Smith 2000; Morrow 2005). That is one reason we conducted the twenty-six interviews. Moreover, "[t]he more variety in the data sources one is able to obtain, the greater will be the richness, breadth, and depth of the data gathered" (Morrow 2005, 256). Thus, we continued to interview until we felt we had a good understanding of the respondents' life experiences. Gradually, themes—and consistency between respondents—began to emerge. The themes became the "race lessons" that the parents taught the adoptees. These lessons are the basis of chapter 4.

As we have noted, we initially thought we might find some resistance or hesitancy regarding the interviews. We nevertheless experienced a warm reception and willingness to talk. We were able to establish the relationships, in part, by noticing things around the home and asking about the hobbies and interests of the families. This was especially easy and important when the individuals being interviewed had family pictures or African art or readings in view. With the recent high-school graduates, we often asked about their future plans and their interests, schools they had attended, and music tastes. As we noted earlier, we believe the adoptive parents' preference in talking to Darron about their experiences was an effort to secure validation and approval from an adult Black male who had grown up in a Black community—someone who was "authentically" Black. They may also have presumed that Darron, as a Black man, would know more about, and confirm, their experiences. As Steinar Kvale (1996, 128) reports, "The subject will want to have a grasp of the interviewer before they allow themselves to talk freely, exposing their experiences and feelings to a stranger." Our respondents seemed to feel that they needed to establish their authenticity as we proceeded in the interviews.

A Note about the Sample

As Donald Polkinghorne (2005, 141) notes, "The purpose of qualitative data is to provide evidence (i.e., to make evident) the characteristics of an experience." Qualitative studies utilize in-depth interviews, often with relatively small sample sizes. As Michael Patton (1990, 184) notes, however, "Sample size depends on what you want to know, the purpose of the inquiry, what's at stake, what will have credibility, and what can be done with available time and resources." Once we were able to discern important patterns and consistency in the interviews, we felt we had achieved closure. The interviews enabled us to construct an in-depth view of the range of experiences and knowledge about transracial adoption and the ways that Black children are racially socialized.

Importantly, theoretical saturation and data redundancy helped us to determine the final number of participants needed for this study (Miles and Huberman 1994). Theoretical saturation was reached when no new concepts, ideas, or dimensions of TRA emerged from several subsequent interviews (Glaser and Strauss 1967; Strauss and Corbin 1990). Similarly, data redundancy was achieved when the interviews repeated patterns or themes already identified (Glaser and Strauss 1967; Strauss and Corbin 1990). We compared interviews with previous ones to examine repeated patterns. And we talked among ourselves, comparing the interviews. When the race stories and lessons recounted by the adoptive parents fit into and matched the existing analytical classification scheme without generating any new topics or themes, we believed that theoretical saturation and data redundancy had been achieved, and we discontinued doing additional interviews.

All together, the transcriptions ran to over four hundred pages. We focused on the race lessons embedded within and conveyed as a result of racial events. These are the experiences that led to the inculcation of race lessons in the adoptees. Participants frequently introduced and elaborated narrative descriptions of racial events to make or underscore a point in their responses to the interview questions.

We identified race lessons by pulling out all segments from transcripts where participants described rules, standards, statements, or expectations about race. Often rules about race and race relations were conveyed within the recounting of the racial events. A transcript segment was identified as a racial event carrying a race lesson if the participant's narrative involved more than a brief example and included at least one of the five dimensions of the White racial frame identified by Leslie Picca and Joe Feagin (2007).

We then coded and sorted the narrative segments by lessons taught. We read each of the protocols individually before coming together to sort racial-event segments and organize them into themes. Differences in respective lists of codes and themes were then used to redefine, challenge, illustrate, and extend the list of themes generated by the separate lists of themes. We trust that we have been honest to the feelings and attitudes of our respondents. These are their stories. We believe that they are best understood as part of the continuing phenomenon of race issues in American society today.

APPENDIX B

Transracial Adoption in the 2000 Census and the National Survey of Adoptive Parents (2007)

HERE WE provide a more detailed examination of the demographic characteristics of those in the nation who have adopted transracially. We present more data from the 2000 census and from the National Survey of Adoptive Parents (NSAP) conducted in 2007. While the census data are now a decade old, the characteristics of those who adopt are not likely to have changed much. The census data represent the first nationally representative sample of families that have adopted transracially. Rose Kreider (2003) presented considerable information about adoption in the 2000 census, but she did not focus on transracial adoption. Prior to the 2000 census, researchers had to rely on small samples of adoptive parents and their transracially adopted children (Alstein and Simon 1977, 1992; Simon et al. 1994; Simon and Roorda 2009; Patton 2000; Jacobson 2008). Large representative samples were simply not available previously.

Using the 5 percent Public Use Micro-data Samples of the census, we first selected those households with children present. This procedure resulted in 4.27 million households. Of these, 103,827 were households in which White parents had adopted children under the age of eighteen present in the home (2.4 percent).[1] Nearly 12 percent (11.7 percent, or 12,110 families) of those households included adopted children who had been identified in the census as Black (or African American), Hispanic, Asian, or other non-White groups. We first present some information about all adoptions before discussing the characteristics of those who adopted transracially.

Table B.1. Sex Ratios for All Adopted Children in the 2000 Census by Groups

Group	*Percent Female*	*Percent Male*
Non-Hispanic White	50.6	49.4
Black	51.6	48.4
Hispanic	51.3	48.7
Asian	63.0	37.0
All others	50.2	49.8

Source: U.S. 2000 Census 5 percent Public Use Micro-data Sample.

Data about All Adoptions in the Census

Three quarters of all adoptees in the census lived with White parents (61.6 percent with two White parents and 12.9 percent with a single White parent). Just over one in five (20.9 percent) lived in minority families (all groups except Whites). Hispanics in the 2000 census were 12.5 percent of the population, African Americans were 12.3 percent, and Asians were about 3.7 percent. Four and a half percent of all adoptees were living in homes where one parent was Black and the other parent White.

Again, as noted in the text, the sex ratio of those adopted was roughly 50 percent male and 50 percent female, with one exception. Sixty-three percent of Asian children who were adopted in the census were female (see table B.1). This is the result of selective adoption from China.

Interestingly, average family size in the census data was identical for those families that adopted and the general population where there was a child in the home (2.3 children per household). All of these results are similar to those reported by Kreider (2003) for children under the age of twenty-five.

Table B.2 shows the breakdown of adoptees by ethnic group, as discussed in chapter 2.

Table B.2. Percentage of Children in Each Group Adopted

Race of Child	*Percentage of Population*	*Percentage Adopted*
White	74.9	2.3
Black	13.7	2.9
Hispanic	16.8	1.8
Asian	4.4	4.2
AIAN (Amer. Indian or Alaskan Native)	2.0	3.5
Native Hawaiian or Pacific Islander	0.4	3.6
Some other race	8.6	1.9

Source: U.S. 2000 Census 5 percent Public Use Micro-data Sample.

Data about Transracial Adoptions in the Census

Table B.3 shows the race of the adoptees in the census who had been adopted by White parents. About a third of all the adoptees were Asian and an additional third Hispanic. Many of the intercountry adoptees were from China and Guatemala, as well as some other Asian and Latin American countries. Black transracial adoptees were the smallest number of all the transracial adoptions. As we note in the text, however, Black transracial adoptions are the most poignant because of historical and lingering racism. The number of adoptions of Asian or Hispanic adoptees by White families was roughly three times that of White families adopting African Americans (see table B.3).

Those who adopted transracially had higher income and educational levels than White families (see table B.4). The White families that adopted Black adoptees had only slightly higher income and educational levels than White adopting families overall. The incomes were less than two thousand dollars more ($80,269, compared to $78,334) for two-parent families, and the educational levels were only slightly higher (11.20 vs. 10.58, where 12 is completion of a college associate's degree). See panel 1 of table B.4. Two-parent White families that had adopted Hispanic and Asian children had substantially higher educational levels (11.64 and 12.19, respectively) when compared to the educational levels of two-parent White families who had their own birth children (10.58).

The analysis yields similar but slightly greater differences for single-parent White families that had adopted transracially. While single-parent families clearly had lower incomes than the two-parent families, the general patterns hold. Single, White parents that had adopted Black children had roughly six thousand dollars higher income than single, White parents who had only their own birth children ($43,034, compared to $37,091). Those that had adopted Hispanic children had eight thousand more in family income ($55,268, compared to $37,091). As with the two-parent families, the single-parent

Table B.3. Transracial Adoptions in the 2000 Census

White Parents with	*Number*	*Percentage*	*Percentage of All Adopted Children*
Hispanic children	3,743	31	1.8
Black children	1,353	11	2.9
Asian children	4,200	35	4.2
"Other" designations*	2,812	23	9.0

Source: U.S. 2000 Census 5 percent Public Use Micro-data Sample.
* Native groups, "other" in census, and two or more races.

Table B.4. Income and Education Comparison of Two-Parent White Families with Transracially Adopted Children

Children	*Average Total Family Income (1999)*	*Education Level of Parent with Highest Level (12 = College Associate's Degree)*
Families with own birth children	$ 78,334	10.58
Adopted Black children	$ 80,269	11.20
Adopted Hispanic children	$103,321	11.64
Adopted Asian children	$110,342	12.19

Source: U.S. 2000 Census 5 percent Public Use Micro-data Sample.
Note: All differences are statistically significant at .05 level or higher.

families who had adopted Asian children had the highest income ($67,939) and educational levels (12.8). The educational levels of those single, White parents who had adopted Hispanic or Black children were also higher than those of single- or two-parent White families.

Results from the National Survey of Adoptive Parents

The results from NSAP data are consistent with the census data. The NSAP is a nationally representative sample of 2,089 adoptive parents. The income data from the NSAP are presented in table B.5. The census and the NSAP use different measures of income: the NSAP measures income in five categories based on poverty levels. Twenty-seven percent of the families that had adopted a same-race child were below 200 percent of the poverty level, but only 14 percent of the families that had adopted transracially fell into the

Table B.5. Income Levels of Transracial Adoptees by Race and Ethnicity, by Percentage of Poverty Level

Race or Ethnicity	*At or Below Poverty Level*	*100–200% Poverty Level*	*200–300% Poverty Level*	*300–400% Poverty Level*	*400% Poverty Level or Above*
Hispanic/Latino	6.1	12.3	14.1	16.2	51.3
White non-Hispanic	6.2	12.7	20.4	14.1	46.6
Black non-Hispanic	18.3	22.5	16.3	13.1	29.7
Asian	0.8	4.6	11.4	18.6	64.6
Other*	14.4	18.5	19.0	10.2	38.0

Source: Derived from National Survey of Adopting Parents.
Note: Differences are statistically significant at the .001 level.
* "Other" includes Pacific Islanders, American Indian, and Alaskan Native, as well as those designating "other."

same levels of income. At the same time, 53 percent of the families that had adopted a same-race child had high incomes (over three times the poverty level), whereas 70.7 percent of the transracial families were in the same high levels of income. In other words, people who had adopted transracially had substantially higher incomes than those parents who had adopted a same-race child.

Whereas 52 percent of the same-race adopters had biological children, only 39 percent of the transracial-adoption families had biological children. And they tended to have younger children. Eighteen percent of the transracial parents had teenagers aged 15–17, compared to 27 percent of the same-race adopters. Conversely, 24 percent of the children of transracial adopters were under age 5, compared to 13 percent of the same-race adopters.

Notes

Chapter 1
Transracial Adoption

1. In this book, we will use the terms *African American*, *Black*, *biracial*, and *African descent* interchangeably to help with flow of the text and narratives. We recognize the complexities obscured by these terms in regard to the multifaceted histories of the peoples represented by these terms. Accordingly, we recognize that these terms tend to invoke and perpetuate images and understandings that often flatten out the richness of particular group histories and the role of power as domination in constraining the abilities of peoples to name and navigate society and the world by and for themselves. Due to space considerations, we use these terms as a shorthand way of referring to monoracial African Americans descended from the heritage of chattel slavery in the United States (as distinct from biraciality as being the mixture of White and Black parents). We also use these terms to refer to children of Black-White biracial heritage.

2. For the protection of individual and family privacy, all names used throughout the text are pseudonyms.

3. We address in later chapters the issues related to stereotypes and assumptions regularly applied to adoptees, for example the idea that compared to males of other racial backgrounds, Black males have larger genitalia and amplified prowess in sexual interactions, and the ways these cultural representations constrain their lives.

Chapter 2
Contextualizing Transracial Adoption

1. For reviews of the increases in interracial marriage, see Kalmijn (1993, 1998), Qian (1997), Heaton and Jacobson (2000), and Kalmijn and Flap (2001).

Chapter 4
Research on Transracial Adoption

1. In this text, we use the abbreviation *TRA* to refer both to the practice of transracial adoption and to an individual who has been transracially adopted.

Chapter 7
Addressing Race with Your Children

1. This is not to suggest that race is not a ubiquitous problem in the United States, or that it is no longer present. Race looks different depending on where you reside. However, in the South, where explosive racism was the focal point of the 1960s racial unrest over full human rights, race relations are and have always been largely a geographical space of outward manifestations of racial difference, where sharp lines have been drawn between Whites and Blacks. In the South, Black and White citizens still know where they stand in relation to one another.

2. Malcolm X made this statement on April 6, 1964, as part of his "Black Revolution" speech at the Hotel Theresa in New York City.

Appendix B
Transracial Adoption in the 2000 Census and the National Survey of Adoptive Parents (2007)

1. We examined only children under the age of eighteen. Thus, our figures differ some from Kreider's (2003), since she included all children living in the household. Our analysis is based on about 75 percent of Kreider's sample.

References

Altstein, H., and Simon, R. J. 1977. Transracial Adoption: An Examination of an American Phenomenon. *Journal of Social Welfare*, 4(2–3), 63–71.

Anderson, L. P. 1991. Acculturative Stress: A Theory of Relevance to Black Americans. *Clinical Psychology Review*, 11, 685–702.

Andujo, E. 1988. Ethnic Identity of Transracially Adopted Hispanic Adolescents. *Social Work*, 33, 531–35.

Angelou, M. 1993. Maya Angelou. In *Discovering Authors* [CD-ROM]. Detroit: Gale Research.

Angrosina, M. V., and Mays de Perez, K. A. 2000. Rethinking Observation. In N. K. Denzin and Y. S. Lincoln, eds., *Handbook of Qualitative Research* (673–702). Thousand Oaks, CA: Sage.

Asante, M. 2003. *Afrocentricity: The Theory of Social Change*. Chicago: African American Images.

Baden, A. L. 2002. The Psychological Adjustment of Transracial Adoptees: An Application of the Cultural/Racial Identity Model. *Journal of Social Distress and the Homeless*, 11, 167–92.

Baldwin, J. 1980, October. *Esquire*, 1.

———. 1985. *The Price of the Ticket: Collected Non-Fiction, 1948–1985*. New York: St. Martin's.

Barkley Brown, E. 1994. Negotiating and Transforming the Public Sphere: African American Political Life in the Transition from Slavery to Freedom. *Public Culture*, 7, 107–46.

Bell, D. 1992. *Faces at the Bottom of the Well: The Permanence of Racism*. New York: Basic Books.

———. 2004. *Silent Covenants*. New York: Oxford University Press.

Bell, L. A. 1997. Theoretical Foundations for Social Justice Education. In M. Adams, L. A. Bell, and P. Griffin, eds., *Teaching for Diversity and Social Justice* (1–15). New York: Routledge.

Bennett, L. 1972. *The Challenge of Blackness*. Chicago: Johnson Publishing Company.

Benson, P., Sharma, A., and Roehlkepartain, E. C. 1994. *Growing Up Adopted: A Portrait of Adolescents and Their Families*. Minneapolis: Search Institute.

Berry, M., Barth, R. P., and Needell, B. 1996. Preparation, Support, and Satisfaction of Adoptive Families in Agency and Independent Adoptions. *Child Adolescent Social Work Journal*, 13, 157–83.

Bhabha, H. 1989. The Commitment to Theory. In J. Pines and P. Williemen, eds., *Third Cinema Reader* (111–32). London: British Film Institute.

Bonilla-Silva, E. 2003. *Racism without Racists: Color-Blind Racism and the Persistence of Racial Inequality in the United States*. New York: Rowman & Littlefield.

Bowman, P. J., and Howard, C. 1985. Race-Related Socialization, Motivation, and Academic Achievement: A Study of Black Youths in Three-Generation Families. *Journal of the American Academy of Child Psychiatry*, 24(2), 131–41.

Boykin, A. W., and Toms, F. 1985. Black Child Socialization: A Conceptual Framework. In H. P. McAdoo and J. L. McAdoo, eds., *Black Children: Social, Educational, and Parental Environments* (33–51). Newbury Park, CA: Sage.

Branch, C. W., and Newcombe, N. 1986. Racial Attitude Development among Young Black Children as a Function of Parental Attitudes: A Longitudinal and Cross-Sectional Study. *Child Development*, 57, 712–21.

Brooks, D., and Barth, R. P. 1999. Adult Transracial and Inracial Adoptees: Effects of Race, Gender, Adoptive Family Structure, and Placement History on Adjustment Outcomes. *American Journal of Orthopsychiatry*, 69, 87–99.

Brooks, M. D. 2001. A Study of the Experiences and Psychosocial Developmental Outcomes of African American Adult Transracial Adoptees. *Dissertation Abstracts International*, 62(1-A), 327.

Brown, T. N., and Lesane-Brown, C. 2006. Race Socialization Messages across Historical Time. *Social Psychology Quarterly*, 69(2), 201–13.

Buckley, P. J., and Carter, M. J. 2004. A Formal Analysis of Knowledge Combination in Multinational Enterprises. *Journal of International Business Studies*, 35, 371–84.

Carter, R. T. 1995. *Race and Racial Identity in Psychotherapy: Toward a Racially Inclusive Model.* New York: Wiley.

Cederblad, M., Hook, B., Irhammar, M., and Mercke, A. 1999. Mental Health in International Adoptees as Teenagers and Young Adults: An Epidemiological Study. *Journal of Child Psychology and Psychiatry and Allied Disciplines*, 40, 1239–48.

Clemetson, L., and Nixon, R. 2006, August 17. Breaking Through Adoption's Racial Barriers. *New York Times.*

Coates, R. D. 2007. Covert Racism in the USA and Globally. *Sociology Compass*, 2, no. 1 (2008), 208–31.

Coffey, A., and Atkinson, P. 1996. *Making Sense of Qualitative Data: Complementary Research Strategies.* Thousand Oaks, CA: Sage.

Comaroff, J. 1993. The Diseased Heart of Africa: Medicine, Colonialism, and the Black Body. In S. Lindenbaum and M. Lock, eds., *Knowledge, Power, and Practice* (39–53). Berkeley: University of California Press.

Cone, J. H. 2004. *Martin and Malcolm and America: A Dream or a Nightmare?* Maryknoll, NY: Orbis.

Cose, E. 1997. *Color-Blind: Seeing beyond Race in a Race-Obsessed World.* New York: HarperCollins.

Cross, W. 1980. Models of Psychological Nigrescence: A Literature Review. In R. L. Jones, ed., *Black Psychology*, 2nd ed. (81–89). New York: Harper and Row.

———. 1985. Black Identity: Rediscovering Distinction between Personal Identity and Reference to Group Orientation. In M. Spencer, G. Brookins, and W. Allen, eds., *Beginnings: The Social and Affective Development of Black Children* (155–71). Hillsdale, NJ: Erlbaum.

———. 1987. A Two-Factor Theory of Black Identity: Implications for the Study of Identity Development in Minority Children. In J. S. Phinney and M. J. Rotherham, eds., *Children's Ethnic Socialization: Pluralism and Development* (117–33). Newbury Park, CA: Sage.

Cross, W., Parham, T. A., and Helms, J. F. 1991. The States of Black Identity Development: Nigrescence Models. In R. Jones, ed., *Black Psychology*, 3rd ed. (319–38). Hampton, VA: Cobb and Henry.

Cross, W., Strauss, L., and P. Fhagen-Smith. 1999. African American Identity Development across the Life Span: Educational Implications. In R.

Hernández Sheets and E. R. Hollins, eds., *Racial and Ethnic Identity in School Practices: Aspects of Human Development* (29–48). Hillsdale, NJ: Erlbaum.

Crowe, C. 2002. *Mississippi Trial, 1955*. New York: Penguin.

Dawson, M. C. 1994. A Black Counterpublic? Economic Earthquakes, Racial Agenda(s), and Black Politics. *Public Culture*, 7, 195–223.

de Anda, D. 1984. Bicultural Socialization: Factors Affecting the Minority Experience. *Social Work*, 29(2), 101–7.

DeBerry, K. M., Scarr, S., and Weinberg, R. 1996. Family Racial Socialization and Ecological Competence: Longitudinal Assessments of African American Transracial Adoptees. *Child Development*, 67, 2375–99.

De Haymes, M. V., and Simon, S. 2003. Transracial Adoption: Families Identify Issues and Needed Support Services. *Child Welfare*, 82(2), 251–72.

Dei, G. J. S., and Johal, G. S. 2005. *Critical Issues in Antiracist Research Methodologies*. New York: Peter Lang.

Demo, D. H., and Hughes, M. 1990. Socialization and Racial Identity among Black Americans. *Social Psychology Quarterly*, 53, 364–74.

Denzin, N. K., and Lincoln, Y. S. 2000. Introduction: The Discipline and Practice of Qualitative Research. In N. K. Denzin and Y. S. Lincoln, eds., *Handbook of Qualitative Research*, 2nd ed. (1–36). Thousand Oaks, CA: Sage.

Diamond, J. 1994, November. Race without Color. *Discover*, 82–89.

Douglass, F. 1852/1972. The Meaning of July Fourth for the Negro. In P. S. Foner ed., *The Voice of Black America: Major Speeches by Negroes in the United States, 1797–1971* (104–29). Thousand Oaks, CA: Sage.

DuBois, W. E. B. 1917/2005. *The Souls of Black Folk*. New York: Pocket Books.

———. 1940/1968. *Dusk of Dawn: An Essay toward an Autobiography of a Race Concept*. New York: Schocken Books.

Eisner, E. W., and Peshkin, A. 1990. *Qualitative Inquiry in Education: The Continuing Debate*. New York: Teachers College Press.

Erickson, E. 1968. *Identity: Youth and Crisis*. New York: Norton.

Fatimilehin, I. A. 1999. Of Jewel Heritage: Racial Socialization and Racial Identity Attitudes amongst Adolescents of Mixed African Caribbean/White Parentage. *Journal of Adolescence*, 22, 303–18.

Feagin, J. 2006. *Systemic Racism: A Theory of Oppression*. New York: Routledge.

———. 2010a. *Racist America*. New York: Routledge.

———. 2010b. *The White Racial Frame: Centuries of Racial Framing and Counterframing*. New York: Routledge.

Feigelman, W. 2000. Adjustments of Transracially Adopted and Inracially Adopted Young Adults. *Child and Adolescent Social Work Journal*, 17, 165–83.

Feigelman, W., and Silverman, A. R. 1984. The Long-Term Effects of Transracial Adoption. *Social Service Review*, 58, 588–602.

Fine, M. 1994. Dis-Stance and Other Stances: Negotiations of Power inside Feminist Research. In A. D. Gitlin, ed., *Power and Method: Political Activism and Educational Research* (13–35). New York: Routledge.

Floyd, S. 1925. *Charming Stories for Young and Old*. Washington, DC: Hertel and Jenkins.

Foner, E. 1990. *A Short History of Reconstruction, 1863–1877*. New York: Harper & Row.

———. 1999. African Americans and American Freedom. *Souls* 1(1), 16–22.

Fontana, A., and Frey, J. H. 2000. The Interview. In N. K. Denzin and Y. S. Lincoln, eds., *Handbook of Qualitative Research*, 2nd ed. (645–72). Thousand Oaks, CA: Sage.

Foucault, M. 1970. *The Order of Things: An Archaeology of the Human Sciences*. New York: Vintage.

———. 1972. *The Archaeology of Knowledge and the Discourse on Language*. A. M. Sheridan Smith, trans. New York: Pantheon.

Franklin, B. 1999. Discourse, Rationality, and Educational Research: A Historical Perspective. *Review of Educational Research*, 69(4), 347–63.

Frasch, K. M., and Brooks, D. 2003. Normative Development in Transracial Adoptive Families: An Integration of the Literature and Implications for the Construction of a Theoretical Framework. *Families in Society: The Journal of Contemporary Human Services*, 84(2), 201–12.

Freundlich, M. 2000. *Adoption and Ethics*, vol. 1. *The Role of Race, Culture, and National Origin in Adoption*. Washington, DC: Child Welfare League of America.

Freundlich, M., and Lieberthal, J. K. 2000. *The Gathering of the First Generation of Adult Korean Adoptees: Adoptees' Perceptions of International Adoption*. New York: Evan B. Donaldson Adoption Institute. At www.adoptioninstitute.org/research/instituteresearch.php (accessed September 17, 2007).

Friedlander, M. L., Larney, L. C., Skau, M., Hotaling, M., Cutting, J. L., and Schwam, M. 2000. Bicultural Identification: Experiences of Internationally Adopted Children and Their Parents. *Journal of Marital and Family Therapy*, 25(1), 43–60.

Gaines, K. K. 1996. *Uplifting the Race: Black Leadership, Politics, and Culture in the Twentieth Century*. Chapel Hill: University of North Carolina Press.

Gitlin, A. D. 1990. Educative Research, Voice, and School Change. *Harvard Educational Review*, 60(4), 443–66.

Glaser, B., and Strauss, A. 1967. *The Discovery of Grounded Theory: Strategies for Qualitative Research.* Chicago: Aldine.

Goldberg, D. T. 1993. *Racist Culture: Philosophy and the Politics of Meaning.* Cambridge, MA: Blackwell.

Gossett, T. F. 1997. *Race: The History of an Idea in America.* New York: Oxford University Press.

Gould, S. J. 1999. *Rock of Ages: Science and Religion in the Fullness of Life.* New York: Ballantine Books.

Greene, B. A. 1990. What Has Gone Before: The Legacy of Racism and Sexism in the Lives of Black Mothers and Daughters. *Women and Therapy*, 9, 207–30.

———. 1992. Racial Socialization as a Tool in Psychotherapy with African American Children. In L. A. Vargas and J. D. Koss-Chioino, eds., *Working with Culture: Psychotherapeutic Interventions with Ethnic Minority Children and Adolescents* (63–81). San Francisco: Jossey-Bass.

Grow, L. J., and Shapiro, D. 1974. *Black Children, White Parents: A Study of Transracial Adoption.* New York: Child Welfare League of America.

Hajal, F., and Rosenberg, E. B. 1991. The Family Life Cycle. *American Journal of Orthopsychiatry*, 61, 78–85.

Hall, H. R. 2007. Poetic Expressions: Students of Color Express Resiliency through Metaphors and Similes. *Journal of Advanced Academics*, 18(2), 216–44.

Haller, J. S. 1995. *Outcasts from Evolution: Scientific Attitudes of Racial Inferiority, 1859–1900.* Urbana: University of Illinois Press.

Harris, V. J. 1992. African-American Conceptions of Literacy: A Historical Perspective. *Theory into Practice*, 31, 276–86.

Heaton, T. B., and Jacobson, C. K. 2000. Intergroup Marriage: An Analysis of Opportunity Structures. *Sociological Inquiry*, 70, 30–41.

Heyman, J. D., and Chiu, A. 2010, May 10. Sandra Bullock: Loving Louis. *People*, 171–82.

Hill, R. 1998. Enhancing the Resilience of African American Families. *Journal of Human Behavior in the Social Environment*, 1(2/3), 49–61.

Hill Collins, P. 2000. *Black Feminist Thought: Knowledge, Consciousness, and the Politics of Empowerment*, 2nd ed. New York: Routledge.

Hjern, A., Lindblad, F., and Vinnerjung, B. 2002. Suicide, Psychiatric Illness, and Social Maladjustment in Intercountry Adoptees in Sweden: A Cohort Study. *Lancet*, 360, 443–48.

Hollingsworth, L. D. 1997. Effect of Transracial/Transethnic Adoption on Children's Racial and Ethnic Identity and Self-Esteem: A Meta-Analytic View. *Marriage and Family Review*, 25, 99–130.

hooks, b. 1990. *Yearning: Race, Gender, and Cultural Politics*. Boston: South End Press.

———. 1995. *Killing Rage: Ending Racism*. New York: Henry Holt.

Hughes, D., and Chen, L. 1999. The Nature of Parents' Race-Related Communications to Children: A Developmental Perspective. In L. Balter and C. S. Tamis-LeMonda, eds., *Child Psychology: A Handbook of Contemporary Issues* (467–90). New York: Psychology Press.

Hughes, D., and Shweder, R. A. 1996. Midlife Development in the United States (Midus): Survey of Minority Groups [Chicago and New York City], 1995–1996, 2nd ICPSR version (digital file). Chicago: Metro Chicago Information Center.

Huh, N. S., and Reid, W. J. 2000. Intercountry, Transracial Adoption and Ethnic Identity. *International Social Work*, 43(1), 75–87.

Jackman, M. 1986. "Some of my best friends are black . . ." Interracial Friendship and Whites' Racial Attitudes. *Public Opinion Quarterly*, 50(4), 459–86.

———. 1994. *The Velvet Glove: Paternalism and Conflict in Gender, Class, and Race Relations*. Berkeley: University of California Press.

———. 1996. Individualism, Self-Interest, and White Racism. *Social Science Quarterly*, 77(4), 760–67.

Jacobson, C. K. 2004. African American Latter-day Saints. In N. Bringhurst and D. T. Smith, eds., *Black and Mormon* (116–32). Urbana: University of Illinois Press.

Jacobson, C. K., and T. B. Heaton. 2008. Comparative Patterns of Interracial Marriage: Structural Opportunities, Third-Party Factors, and Temporal Changes. *Journal of Comparative Family Studies*, 39, 129–49.

Jacobson, H. 2008. *Culture Keeping: White Mothers, International Adoption, and the Negotiation of Family Difference*. Nashville: Vanderbilt University Press.

Johnson, B. R., and Jacobson, C. K. 2005. Contact in Context: An Examination of Social Settings on Whites' Attitudes toward Interracial Marriage. *Social Psychology Quarterly*, 68, 387–99.

Johnson, P. R., Shireman, J. F., and Watson, K. W. 1987. Transracial Adoption and the Development of Black Identity at Age Eight. *Child Welfare*, 66, 45–55.

Jordan, G., and Weedon, C. 1995. *Cultural Politics: Class, Gender, Race, and the Postmodern World*. Malden, MA: Blackwell.

Jordan, W. D. 1974. *The White Man's Burden*. New York: Oxford University Press.

Joseph, P. E. 2001. Black Reconstructed: White Supremacy in Post Civil Rights America. *Black Scholar*, 25(4), 52–55.

Juffer, F. 2006. Children's Awareness of Adoption and Their Problem Behavior in Families with 7-Year-Old Internationally Adopted Children. *Adoption Quarterly*, 9(2/3), 1–22.

Kallgren, C. A., and Caudill, P. J. 1993. Current Transracial Adoption Practices: Racial Dissonance or Racial Awareness? *Psychological Reports*, 72, 551–58.

Kalmijn, M. 1993. Trends in Black/White Intermarriage. *Social Forces*, 72, 119–46.

———. 1998. Intermarriage and Homogamy: Causes, Patterns, and Trends. *Annual Review of Sociology*, 24, 395–421.

Kalmijn, M., and Flap, H. D. 2001. Assortative Meeting and Mating: Unintended Consequences of Organized Settings for Partner Choices. *Social Forces*, 79, 1289–1319.

Keith, M. V., and Herring, C. 1991. Skin Tone Stratification in the Black Community. *American Journal of Sociology*, 97, 760–80.

Kelley, R. D. G. 1997. *Yo' Mama's Disfunktional: Fighting the Culture Wars in Urban America*. Boston: Beacon Press.

Kenney, K. 1999. Multiracial Families. In *Advocacy in Counseling: Counselors, Clients, and Community* (chapter 6). Document ED 435 910. Available through ERIC Counseling and Student Services Clearinghouse.

Kerwin, C., Ponterotto, J. G., Jackson, B. L., and Harris, A. 1993. Racial Identity in Biracial Children: A Qualitative Investigation. *Journal of Counseling Psychology*, 40(2), 221–31.

Kim, D. S. 1977. How They Fared in American Homes: A Follow-Up Study of Adopted Korean Children in the United States. *Children Today*, 6, 2–6.

Kinnamon, K., and Fabre, M., eds. 1993. *Conversations with Richard Wright*. Jackson: University Press of Mississippi.

Kluegel, J. R., and E. R. Smith. 1986. *Beliefs about Inequality: Americans' Views of What Is and What Ought to Be*. New York: Aldine de Gruyter.

Kreider, R. M. 2003. Adopted Children and Stepchildren: 2000 (U.S. Census Special Report). U.S. Department of Commerce, Economics and Statistics Administration.

Krysan, M., and Lewis, A. E. 2004. *The Changing Terrain of Race and Ethnicity*. New York: Russell Sage Foundation.

Kunjufu, J. 1995. *Countering the Conspiracy to Destroy Black Boys*. Chicago: African American Images.

Kvale, S. 1996. *InterViews: An Introduction to Qualitative Research Interviewing*. Thousand Oaks, CA: Sage.

Lee, R. M. 2003. The Transracial Adoption Paradox: History, Research, and Counseling Implications of Cultural Socialization. *Counseling Psychologist*, 31(6), 711–44.

Leonardo, Z. 2009. *Race, Whiteness, and Education*. New York: Routlege.

Lipsitz, G. 2006. *The Possessive Investment in Whiteness: How White People Profit from Identity Politics*, 2nd ed. Philadelphia: Temple University Press.

Lopez, I. 2006. Colorblind to the Reality of Race in America. *Chronicle of Higher Education*, 53(11), B6.

Lorde, A. 1984. *Sister Outsider: Essays and Speeches*. Freedom, CA: Crossing Press.

Lovelock, K. 2000. Intercountry Adoption as a Migratory Practice: A Comparative Analysis of Intercountry Adoption and Immigration Policy and Practice in the United States, Canada and New Zealand in the Post W.W. II Period. *International Migration Review*, 34, 907–49.

Lunneborg, P. 1999. *The Chosen Lives of Childfree Men*. Westport, CT: Bergin and Garvey.

Marable, M. 1993. Beyond Racial Identity Politics: Towards a Liberation Theory for Multicultural Democracy. *Race and Class*, 35(1), 113–30.

———. 1995. *Beyond Black and White: Transforming African American Politics*. New York: Verso.

Marshall, S. 1995. Ethnic Socialization of African American Children: Implications of Parenting, Identity Development, and Academic Achievement. *Journal of Youth and Adolescence*, 24(4), 377–96.

Mauss, A. 2004. Casting Off the "Curse of Cain": The Extent and Limits of Progress since 1978. In N. Bringhurst and D. T. Smith, eds., *Black and Mormon* (82–116). Urbana: University of Illinois Press.

McAdoo, H. P. 2002. *Black Children: Social, Educational, and Parental Environments*. Thousand Oaks, CA: Sage.

McRoy, R. G. 1989. An Organizational Dilemma: The Case of Transracial Adoption. *Journal of Applied Behavioral Science*, 25, no. 2 (May), 145–60.

———. 1994. Racial Identity and Attachment in Transracial Adoptions: Implications for Child Placement Decision-Making. *Journal of Multicultural Social Work*, 3, 59–75.

McRoy, R. G., and Grape, H. 1999. Skin Color in Transracial and Inracial Adoptive Placements: Implications for Special Needs Adoptions. *Child Welfare*, 78(5), 673–92.

McRoy, R. G., and Zurcher, L. A. 1983. *Transracial and Inracial Adoptees*. Springfield, IL: Charles Thomas.

Merriam, S. B. 2001. *Qualitative Research and Case Study Applications in Education: Revised and Expanded from "Case Study Research in Education."* San Francisco: Jossey-Bass.

Miles, M. B., and Huberman, A. M. 1994. *An Expanded Sourcebook: Qualitative Data Analysis*, 2nd ed. Thousand Oaks, CA: Sage.

Mills, C. 1997. *The Racial Contract.* Ithaca, NY: Cornell University Press.

Mohanty, J., Keokse, G., and Sales, E. 2006. Family Cultural Socialization, Ethnic Identity, and Self-Esteem: Web-Based Survey of International Adult Adoptees. *Journal of Ethnic and Cultural Diversity in Social Work*, 15(3–4), 153–72.

Moore, E. G. J. 1987. Ethnic Social Milieu and Black Children's Intelligence Test Achievement. *Journal of Negro Education*, 56, 44–110.

Morrow, S. L. 2005. Quality and Trustworthiness in Qualitative Research in Counseling Psychology. *Journal of Counseling Psychology*, 52(2), 250–60.

Morrow, S. L., and Smith, M. L. 2000. Qualitative Research for Counseling Psychology. In S. D. Brown and R. W. Lent, eds., *Handbook of Counseling Psychology*, 3rd ed. (199–230). New York: Wiley.

Munford, C. J. 1996. *Race and Reparations: A Black Perspective for the Twenty-first Century*. Trenton, NJ: Africa World Press.

National Association of Black Social Workers. 1972. Position Statement on Trans-Racial Adoption. At www.uoregon.edu/~adoption/archive/NabswTRA.htm (accessed May 27, 2008).

Ogbu, J. 1985. A Cultural Ecology of Competence among Inner-City Blacks. In M. Spencer, G. Brookins, and W. Allen, eds., *Beginnings: The Social and Affective Development of Black Children* (45–66). Hillsdale, NJ: Erlbaum.

Olson, J. 2004. *The Abolition of White Democracy*. Minneapolis: University of Minnesota Press.

Omi, M., and Winant, H. 1994. *Racial Formation in the United States: From the 1960s to the 1980s*. New York: Routledge.

Parham, T.A., and Helms, J. E. 1981. The Influence of Black Students' Racial Identity Attitudes on Preferences for Counselor's Race. *Journal of Counseling Psychology*, 28, 250–57.

Patton, M. Q. 1990. *Qualitative Evaluation and Research Methods*, 2nd ed. Newbury Park, CA: Sage.

Patton, S. 2000. *Birth Marks: Transracial Adoption in Contemporary America.* New York: New York University Press.

Pertman, A. 2000. *Adoption Nation: How the Adoption Revolution Is Transforming America.* New York: Basic Books.

Peters, M. F. 1985. Racial Socialization of Young Black Children. In H. P. McAdoo and J. L. McAdoo, eds., *Black Children: Social, Educational, and Parental Environments* (159–73). Newbury Park, CA: Sage.

Phinney, J. S. 1989. Stages of Ethnic Identity Development in Minority Group Adolescents. *Journal of Early Adolescence*, 9, 34–49.

———. 1991. Ethnic Identity and Self-Esteem: A Review and Integration. *Hispanic Journal of Behavioral Sciences*, 13(2), 193–208.

Phinney, J. S., Cantu, C. L., and Kurtz, D. A. 1997. Ethnic and American Identity as Predictors of Self-Esteem among African American, Latino, and White Adolescents. *Journal of Youth and Adolescence*, 26, 165–85.

Picca, L. H., and Feagin, J. 2007. *Two-Faced Racism: Whites in the Backstage and Frontstage*. New York: Routledge.

Pinderhughes, E. 1995. Empowering Diverse Populations: Family Practice in the Twenty-first Century. *Families in Society*, 76(3), 131–40.

Poindexter-Cameron, J. A., and Robinson, T. L. 1997. Relationships among Racial Identity Attitudes, Womanist Identity Attitudes, and Self-Esteem in African American College Women. *Journal of College Student Development*, 38, 288–96.

Polkinghorne, D. E. 1995. Narrative Configuration in Qualitative Analysis. *Qualitative Studies in Education*, 8(1), 5–23.

———. 2005. Language and Meaning: Data Collection in Qualitative Research. *Journal of Counseling Psychology*, 52, 137–45.

Pollack, W. S. 2005. Sustaining and Reframing Vulnerability and Connection: Creating Genuine Resilience in Boys and Young Males. In S. Goldstein and R. B. Brooks, eds., *Handbook of Resilience in Children* (65–77). New York: Springer.

Ponterotto, J. G. 2005. Qualitative Research in Counseling Psychology: A Primer on Research Paradigms and Philosophy of Science. *Journal of Counseling Psychology*, 52, 126–36.

Popkewitz, T. S., and Brennan, M. 1998. *Foucault's Challenge: Discourse, Knowledge, and Power in Education*. New York: Teachers College Press.

Poston, W. S. C. 1990. The Biracial Identity Development Model: A Needed Addition. *Journal of Counseling and Development*, 69(2), 152–55.

Qian, Z. 1997. Breaking the Racial Barriers: Variations in Interracial Marriage between 1980 and 1990. *Demography*, 34, 478–500.

Raible, J. 1990. The Significance of Racial Identity in Transracially Adopted Young Adults. At nysccc.org/family-supports/transracial-transcultural/voices-of-adoptees/the-significance-of-racial-identity/ (accessed August 16, 2007).

Readers: Children Learn Attitudes about Race at Home. 2010, May 19. At articles.cnn.com/2010-05-19/us/doll.study.reactions_1_black-children-white-children-race?_s=PM:US; (accessed June 17, 2011).

Reinharz, S. 1992. *Feminist Methods in Social Research*. New York: Oxford University Press.

Roediger, D. R. 1999. *The Wages of Whiteness: Race and the Making of the American Working Class*. New York: Verso.

———. 2002. *Colored White: Transcending the Racial Past*. Berkeley: University of California Press.

Root, M. P. P. 1990. Resolving "Other" Status: Identity Development of Biracial Individuals. *Women and Therapy*, 9(1–2), 185–205.

Rose, N. 1989. *Governing the Soul*. New York: Free Association Books.

Rothenberg, P. S. 2002. *White Privilege: Essential Readings on the Other Side of Racism*. New York: Worth.

Rotheram, M. J., and Phinney, J. S. 1987. Introduction: Definitions and Perspectives in the Study of Children's Ethnic Socialization. In J. S. Phinney and M. J. Rotheram, eds., *Children's Ethnic Socialization: Pluralism and Development* (10–28). Newbury Park, CA: Sage.

Rush, S. 2000. *Loving across the Color Line: A White Adoptive Mother Learns about Race*. Lanham, MD: Rowman & Littlefield.

Saint-Aubin, A. F. 2002. A Grammar of Black Masculinity: A Body of Science. *Journal of Men's Studies*, 10(3), 247–70.

Samuels, G. M. 2009. "Being Raised by White People": Navigating Difference among Adopted Multiracial Adults. *Journal of Marriage and Family*, 71, 80–94.

Sanders-Thompson, V. L. 1994. Socialization to Race and Its Relationship to Racial Identification among African Americans. *Journal of Black Psychology*, 20(2), 175–88.

Scarr, S., Weinberg, R. A., and Waldman, I. D. 1993. IQ Correlations in Transracial Adoptive Families. *Intelligence*, 17, 541–55.

Scott, J. 1992. Multiculturalism and the Politics of Identity. *October*, 61(1), 12–19.

Sears, D. O., Sidanius, J., and Bobo, L. 2000. *Racialized Politics: The Debate about Racism in America*. Chicago: University of Chicago Press.

Silverman, A. R. 1993. Outcomes of Transracial Adoption, *The Future of Children: Adoption 3*, 104–8.

Simon, R. J., and Altstein, H. 1987. *Transracial Adoptees and Their Families: A Study of Identity and Commitment*. New York: Praeger.

———. 1992. *Adoption, Race, and Identity: From Infancy through Adolescence*. New York: Praeger.

———. 2000. *Adoption across Borders: Serving the Children in Transracial and Intercountry Adoptions*. New York: Rowman & Littlefield.

Simon, R. J., Altstein, H., and M. S. Melli. 1994. *The Case for Transracial Adoption*. Washington, DC: American University Press.

Simon, R. J., and Roorda, R. M. 2009. *In Their Siblings' Voices: White Non-Adopted Siblings Talk about Their Experiences Being Raised with Black and Biracial Brothers and Sisters*. New York: Columbia University Press.

Smith, S., McRoy, R. G., Freundlich, M., and Kroll, J. 2008. *Finding Families for African American Children: The Role of Race and Law in Adoption from Foster Care*. New York: Evan B. Donaldson Adoption Institute.

Speight, S. L., Vera, E. M., and Derrickson, K. B. 1996. Racial Self-Designation, Racial Identity, and Self-Esteem Revisted. *Journal of Black Psychology*, 22, 37–52.

Spelman, E. 1988. *Inessential Woman: Problems of Exclusion in Feminist Thought*. Boston: Beacon Press.

Spencer, M. 1988. Self-Concept Development. In D. T. Slaughter, ed., *Perspectives on Black Child Development: New Directions for Child Development* (59–72). San Francisco: Jossey-Bass.

Stevenson, H. C., Jr. 1993. Validation of the Scale of Race Socialization for African American Adolescents: A Preliminary Analysis. *Psychology Discourse*, 24(12), 7–12.

Strauss, A., and Corbin, J. 1990. *Basics of Qualitative Research: Grounded Theory Procedures and Techniques*. Thousand Oaks, CA: Sage.

Suzuki, L. A., Ahluwalia, M. K., Arora, A. K., and Mattis, S. J. 2007. The Pond You Fish In Determines the Fish You Catch: Exploring Strategies for Qualitative Data Collection. *Counseling Psychologist*, 35(2), 295–327.

Tatum, B. D. 2004. Family Life and School Experience: Factors in the Racial Identity Development of Black Youth in White Communities. *Journal of Social Issues*, 60, 117–35.

Thomas, A. J., and Speight, S. L. 1999. Racial Identity and Racial Socialization Attitudes of African American Parents. *Journal of Black Psychology*, 25(2), 152–70.

Thomas, K. A., and Tessler, R. C. 2007. Bicultural Socialization among Adoptive Families. *Journal of Family Issues*, 28(9), 1189–1219.

Thompson, B., and Tyagi, S. 1996. *Names We Call Home: Autobiography on Racial Identity*. New York: Routledge.

Thompson, C. P., Anderson, L. P., and Bakeman, R. A. 2000. Effects of Racial Socialization and Racial Identity on Acculturative Stress in African American College Students. *Culture Diversity and Ethnic Minority Psychology*, 6(2), 196–210.

Thornton, M. C. 1997. Strategies of Racial Socialization among Black Parents: Mainstream, Minority, and Cultural Messages. In R. J. Taylor, J. S. Jackson, and L. M. Chatters, eds., *Family Life in Black America* (201–15). Thousand Oaks, CA: Sage.

Thornton, M. C., Chatters, L. M., Taylor, R. J., and Allen, W. R. 1990. Sociodemographic and Environmental Correlates of Racial Socialization by Black Parents. *Child Development*, 61, 401–9.

Twine, F. W. 1997. Brown-skinned White Girls: Class, Culture, and the Construction of White Identity in Suburban Communities. In R. Frankenberg, ed., *Displacing Whiteness: Essays in Social and Cultural Criticism* (214–43). Durham, NC: Duke University Press.

Van Ausdale, D., and Feagin, J. 2001. *The First R: How Children Learn Race and Racism*. New York: Rowman & Littlefield.

Vandivere, S., Malm, K., and Radel, L. 2009. *Adoption USA: A Chartbook Based on the 2007 National Survey of Adoptive Parents*. Washington, DC: U.S. Department of Health and Human Services, Office of the Assistant Secretary for Planning and Evaluation.

Vittrup, B. 2009. What U.S. Parents Don't Know about Their Children's Television Use: Discrepancies between Parents' and Children's Reports. *Journal of Children and Media*, 3(1), 51–67.

Ward, J. V. 1990. Racial Identity Formation and Transformation. In C. Gilligan, N. Lyons, and T. J. Hamner, eds., *Making Connections* (215–32). Cambridge, MA: Harvard University Press.

Weedon, C. 1997. *Feminist Practice and Poststructuralist Theory*. New York: Blackwell.

———. 1999. *Feminism, Theory, and the Politics of Difference*. New York: Blackwell.

Weinberg, R.A., Waldman, I., van Dulmen, M. H. M., and Scarr, S. 2004. The Minnesota Transracial Adoption Study: Parent Reports of Psychological Adjustment at Late Adolescence. *Adoption Quarterly*, 8(2), 27–43.

West, T. R. 2002. *Signs of Struggle: The Rhetorical Politics of Cultural Difference*. Albany: State University of New York Press.

Westhues, A., and Cohen, J. S. 1998. Racial and Ethnic Identity of Internationally Adopted Adolescents and Young Adults: Some Issues in Relation to Children's Rights. *Adoption Quarterly*, 1, 33–55.

Williams Willing, I. A. 2004. The Adopted Vietnamese Community: From Fairy Tales to the Diaspora. *Michigan Quarterly Review*, 43 (Fall), 4.

Wise, T. 2009. *Between Barack and a Hard Place: Racism and White Denial in the Age of Obama*. San Francisco: City Lights.

Witzig, R. 1996. The Medicalization of Race: Scientific Legitimization of a Flawed Social Construct. *Annals of Internal Medicine*, 125(8), 675–79.

Wolfe, P. 2002. Race and Racialization: Some Thoughts. *Postcolonial Studies*, 5(1), 51–62.

Wright, R. 1957. *White Man, Listen!* Garden City, NY: Anchor Books.

Yancey, G. 2004. *What White Looks Like: African American Philosophers on the Whiteness Question*. New York: Routledge.

Yoon, D. P. 2001. Causal Modeling Predicting Psychological Adjustment of Korean-Born Adolescent Adoptees. *Journal of Human Behavior in the Social Environment*, 3, 65–82.

Zamostny, K. P., O'Brien, K. M., Baden, A. L., and O'Leary Wiley, M. 2003. The Practice of Adoption: History, Trends, and Social Context. *Counseling Psychologist*, 31, 651–78.

Zelizer, V. A. 1985. *Pricing the Priceless Child: The Changing Social Value of Children*. Princeton, NJ: Princeton University Press.

Index

Note: Page numbers given in *italics* indicate tables.

About the Authors

Darron T. Smith is assistant professor in the College of Health Professions at Wichita State University. He has lectured and published widely in the fields of race, gender, class, and religious studies. He is a frequent commentator on American race relations and has been featured in numerous media outlets, including ESPN's *Outside the Line*, the *New York Times*, and the *Chicago Tribune*. Dr. Smith's April 2011 sports blog posted on Deadspin.com regarding the Brigham Young University honor-code controversy has to date received over 200,000 hits. He is coeditor of the book *Black and Mormon* (with Newell G. Bringhurst).

Cardell K. Jacobson is Karl G. Maser Professor of General Education and professor of sociology at Brigham Young University. He did his graduate work at the University of North Carolina at Chapel Hill, where he acquired his first interest in race and ethnic relations. He teaches and does research on race and ethnic relations, interracial marriage, transracial adoption, social psychology, attitudes and attitude change, and sociology of religion. He has also taught at University of Wisconsin–Milwaukee and Central Michigan University. His last two books were *Modern Polygamy in the United States: Historical, Cultural and Legal Issues* (edited with Lara Burton) and *Within the Social World: Essays in Social Psychology* (edited with Jeffrey C. Chin).

Brenda G. Juárez is assistant professor of social justice education at the University of Massachusetts Amherst. She is a former teacher with a background in teaching within both public- and private-school settings, as well as within business settings, developing curriculum for, and teaching English as a second language to, adult learners. Since joining the professorate, she has continued to develop and expand her interest in issues of social justice and explore what it means to be and to become a full participant in or citizen of a community. She previously taught at Brigham Young University and at the University of South Alabama. Dr. Juárez has organized and helped to facilitate self-directed student groups such as the Future Teachers for Freedom Dreams. Her research has appeared in journals such as *Democracy and Education*, *Journal of Black Studies*, *Race Ethnicity and Education*, *Power and Education*, and *International Journal of Qualitative Studies in Education.*